AMSTERDAM
Hanover
BERLIN
ETHERLANDS

GERMANY

Cologne
Leipzig
UM
Coblenz
ELS
Bastogne
Mainz • Frankfurt
PRAGUE
LUX • Trier
• Bad-Kreuznach
Verdun
• Worms
Kaiserslautern
Nuremburg
SLOVAKIA
Ions
Metz
• Karlsruhe
Nancy
Stuttgart
HUNGARY
Munich
VIENNA

Bern
SWITZERLAND

Lyon
Venice
CROATIA
MILAN

• Genova
SERBIA
Nice
Florence
ITALY
MONTENEGRO
rseille
ROME
Corsica
na
ALBANIA
Naples
sles
Sardinia

Palermo
erranean Sea
Sicily

TUNIS
Malta
TUNISIA

Scale of Miles

50   0   200

N

GENERAL GEORGE PATTON
OLD BLOOD & GUTS

General George Patton

GENERAL GEORGE PATTON
OLD BLOOD & GUTS

ALDEN HATCH

STERLING PUBLISHING CO., INC.
New York

WITH MANY THANKS

It is my best hope that those who read this book will enjoy that experience a fraction as much as I enjoyed writing it. The career of General George S. Patton, Jr., was so full of color and flash, yet his character was so genuine, inspired as it was by those twin virtues, courage and integrity, that living with his memory in the intimacy of author and subject was a time of pure delight.

Not the least pleasurable part of this experience was knowing and working with General Patton's family and loyal friends who cooperated with me in the true Patton spirit of always doing a thing all out.

I am particularly indebted to Mrs. George S. Patton, Jr., and her daughter, Mrs. John C. Waters, who not only furnished me with many hitherto unpublished details of the General's family and military life, but read the manuscript with meticulous care to check it for factual inaccuracies.

Others who supplied first-hand information and comment were: General of the Army, Dwight D. Eisenhower and Mrs. Eisenhower, Miss Anita Patton, Mr. Joseph Banning, Col. Paul D. Harkins, Col. John C. Waters, Lieut. Col. William C. Proctor, Patrick Mitchell, and many others.

In addition I have drawn heavily on the following books: *"War As I Knew It,"* by General George S. Patton, Jr., *"Lucky Forward,"* by Col. Robert S. Allen, *"Crusade in Europe,"* by Dwight D. Eisenhower, *"Patton—Fighting Man,"* by William Bancroft Meller, and *"General George S. Patton, Jr.,"* by James Wellard.

ALDEN HATCH
May 30, 1950

"Somerleas," Cedarhurst, Long Island

A FLYING POINT PRESS BOOK

Design: PlutoMedia
Front cover photograph: Getty Images
Back cover and frontispiece photograph: National Archives

Library of Congress Cataloging-in-Publication Data

Hatch, Alden, 1898-
General George Patton : Old Blood and Guts / Alden Hatch.
p. cm. — (Sterling point books)
Includes index.
ISBN-13: 978-1-4027-3186-0
ISBN-10: 1-4027-3186-8
1. Patton, George S. (George Smith), 1885-1945—Juvenile literature. 2. Generals—United States—Biography—Juvenile literature. 3. United States. Army—Biography—Juvenile literature. 4. United States—History, Military—20th century—Juvenile literature. 5. World War, 1939-1945—Campaigns—Juvenile literature. I. Title. II. Series.

E745.P3H32 2005
355.0092—dc22

2005026768

2 4 6 8 10 9 7 5 3 1

Published by Sterling Publishing Co., Inc.
387 Park Avenue South, New York, NY 10016
Original edition published by Julian Messner, Inc.
under the title *George Patton: The General Wore Spurs*
Copyright © 1950 by Allene Gaty Hatch
New material in this updated edition
Copyright © 2006 by Flying Point Press
Maps copyright © by Richard Thompson, Creative Freelancers, Inc.
Distributed in Canada by Sterling Publishing
c/o Canadian Manda Group, 165 Dufferin Street
Toronto, Ontario, Canada M6K 3H6
Distributed in the United Kingdom by GMC Distribution Services
Castle Place, 166 High Street, Lewes, East Sussex, England BN7 1XU
Distributed in Australia by Capricorn Link (Australia) Pty. Ltd.
P.O. Box 704, Windsor, NSW 2756, Australia

Printed in China
All rights reserved

Sterling ISBN-13: 978-1-4027-3186-0
ISBN-10: 1-4027-3186-8

For information about custom editions, special sales, premium and corporate purchases, please contact Sterling Special Sales Department at 800-805-5489 or specialsales@sterlingpub.com.

CONTENTS

GENERAL GEORGE PATTON
OLD BLOOD & GUTS

THE CAMP
IN THE FOREST

COMBAT COMMAND CCB, THE ADVANCE POINT OF Third Army, rattled and clanked through the somber Thüringer Wald late in April, 1945. Tanks, mobile guns, jeeps, truckloads of armored infantry, ambulances, and miscellaneous transport stretched back along the steep, straight road between the towering trees like a loosely articulated, mile-long dragon. The din of motors and the clashing of metal were a shattering accompaniment to their steady progress through the heart of the famous German forest.

At the crest of a hill, a jeep, scouting ahead, stopped abruptly and the officer in it raised his hand. The dragon halted, snorting. Colonel Wesley M. Yale, commanding CCB, ordered his jeep out of line and sped forward to reconnoiter. When he

3

reached the ridge the trees thinned out, leaving a clear view of the valley ahead. Perhaps half a mile away and some hundreds of feet below, lay a great encampment. Row on row of barracks were interspersed with flat parade grounds, and the whole was ringed by machine guns in pillboxes.

Colonel Yale shouted orders into his radio. Tanks and mobile guns lumbered forward and deployed along the ridge. Infantrymen leaped from their trucks and formed a firing line. As each vehicle reached its assigned position, its engine was shut off to save precious gas. The turret guns of the tanks swung noiselessly, pointing down to blast the valley. For an instant everything was frozen immobile on the brink of action. In that tremendous silence Colonel Yale raised his hand, to give the command to fire, and stayed it in mid-course.

A weird rhythmic sound rose from the valley—the beat of human voices chanting in unison. At first the words were indistinguishable; then suddenly they came clear and loud, lifted up through the trees six thousand voices strong:

> *"Georgie Patton, come and get us!*
> *Georgie Patton, set us free!*
> *Georgie Patton, come and get us!*
> *Georgie Patton, set us free!*
> *Georgie Patton, come and get us!*
> *Georgie Patton, set us free!"*

French and English, Russians and Poles, Dutchmen and Belgians and Norwegians, as well as Americans, were confined in that great Nazi prison camp, but the Yanks had taught their fellow prisoners the words of their chant, and together they called on the almost mythical American warrior to rescue them.

The words were sharply defined now; the chant came faster and faster in an urgent crescendo.

> *"Georgie Patton, come and get us!*
> *Georgie Patton, set us free!"*

Suddenly Colonel Yale shouted, "What are waiting for?"—and swung his arm.

A hundred motors exploded into life, a hundred vehicles jumped forward. Down the hill they careened—tanks and trucks and jeeps and guns, all mixed up in one wild scramble to the rescue of their comrades in arms.

The incident in the Thüringer Wald was not unique. All over Germany, when they heard the sound of a rescuing column, Allied prisoners broke into that chant to Georgie Patton. It mattered not if Patton were five hundred miles away. The advancing Allies might be First Army or Ninth or Seventh, Montgomery's British or LeClerc's French; always the prisoners called on Georgie Patton and, as the American armor roared up, the waiting men half expected to see that stern spare figure with the ice-gray eyes, the six-guns swinging at his hips and the stars glittering on his helmet, step from the leading tank. Sometimes they did at that!

For Georgie Patton, during his lifetime, was both devastatingly real and a legendary folk hero, the symbol of victory to Americans, everywhere, and of terror to the Nazis.

CHAPTER 1

LAKE VINEYARD

GEORGIE PATTON WAS UP A TREE. IT WAS A SPLENDID walnut tree with limbs as symmetrical as the treads of a stepladder. From its upper branches he could survey his whole world. Close behind him was the long, low adobe ranch house with its big veranda and many long windows. Farther back was the wild ravine that rustled at night with animal noises. In front of him the ground sloped down to a great plain that stretched toward the Sierra Madre Mountains, floating in ever-changing splendor on the edge of infinity.

The ranch house stood in a small forest, for Grandfather Wilson had loved trees. There were pines and deodars, cottonwoods, pepper trees, eucalyptus, acacias, cedars and tall Italian cypresses, standing like giant soldiers at attention along the ridge. Beyond the trees were acres of vineyards and the dark green, gold-dappled new orange groves. To the right the sun flashed on miniature Lake Wilson.

Everything the thin blond boy could see, from the wooded hill behind him almost to the mountain wall, belonged to his family. For in the year 1890 Lake Vineyard, comprising more than eighteen hundred acres in the San Gabriel Valley, covered most of what is nowadays the cities of Pasadena and San Marino.

Georgie, in his tree, was not particularly interested in the details of the vast domain which his spectacular grandfather had bequeathed to his father and mother. He was scouting the country for enemies, and, unexpectedly, he saw someone. On the tawny plain appeared a cloud of dust and, in front of it, Georgie's keen gray eyes detected a wildly galloping horseman. He scrambled quickly down the tree, dropped the last six feet, and ran into the house.

"Papa! Mama! Somebody's coming! A horsemen riding hard."

Mr. Patton put down a beautifully bound copy of Dante's *Inferno* and followed his excited son out to the veranda, while Mrs. Patton leaned from an upper window.

"It looks like a messenger," Father said. "Can you make him out, dear?"

"I think it's one of Uncle Captain's vaqueros," Mrs. Patton answered. "Probably announcing a visit."

She was proved right when the dusty horsemen clattered up to the steps and shouted, "The Señor Captain he come, with friends."

"Many friends?" asked Georgie's mother.

The Mexican nodded emphatically. "Mucho, mucho!"

"Bueno," said Mr. Patton, and returned to his book.

Georgie's mother flew to the outside kitchen to get the servants started on the gargantuan feast the occasion required, while Georgie ran to tell the news to his sister Nita, and his friend Natio, son of the estate manager, whose father had come to California with Don Benito Wilson long ago.

The three children climbed the walnut tree and presently saw another column of dust rising from the plain. It moved toward them very slowly until it was so near that they could clearly see the splendid Concord coach, drawn by six black pacers, that Captain William Banning loved to drive. Georgie expectantly watched the slim figure sitting very erect on the box and, when the coach was perhaps a quarter of a mile from the house, he saw Captain Banning crack his whip in the lead team's ears. The horses jumped forward and came toward the ranch house at a run, with the coach leaping along behind them over the dusty, rutted road.

With his six horses still at full stretch, Captain Banning

swung the circle in front of the veranda and pulled up short with sparks flying, horses plunging, Mexican footmen leaping off and frantically grabbing at bridles. Passengers clambered hastily off the top of the coach and spilled from its interior. There were Hancock and Joseph Banning with their wives and assorted children, some friends of Uncle Captain from his home at Wilmington, and a few unidentified strangers who had apparently come along for the ride.

For the next two days Lake Vineyard was in a state of continuous fiesta. At night the long table was a sight to see, with a roast turkey at one end, boiled fowls at the other, and a magnificent ham strategically placed at the center. Every available inch of surface was covered with side dishes of vegetables, fruits, gravy, jellies, and huge bowls of ripe olives. All the food and the sparkling wine was grown on the ranch.

Georgie and Nita stayed up late every night—there was no use going to bed, since the noise of singing and feasting made it impossible to sleep anyway. The little boy sat very quietly in a corner of the room listening to Captain Banning's tall tales of his seafaring days and of the time when his father, Phineas Banning, drove stage from San Pedro clear to Chihuahua in Mexico. It was even better when the men began to reminisce about Don Benito.

Georgie's grandfather, Benjamin Davis Wilson—respectfully called Don Benito by the Spaniards—had come to California in 1841, before the Gold Rush. He bought Lake Vineyard from the widow of an earlier settler and made it prosper. He also moved in on local politics and became Alcalde of the little Pueblo de Nuestra Señora la Reine de los Angeles de Parciuncula. A few years later, when Mexico ceded California to the United States, Don Benito changed his title—but not his office—to Mayor of Los Angeles.

Georgie knew by heart all the fantastic stories about his grandfather, but he loved to hear them again and again. His father and the Bannings told of the Gold Rush days in Los Angeles, when Don Benito, acting as his own sheriff, put on his "killing clothes"—a black frock coat and a white linen vest—and went out to convince the lawless founders of the first families of California that he was the quickest man on the draw south of Frisco.

Don Benito's favorite sport was roping grizzly bears, and one weekend he and a group of friends lassoed thirty of these ferocious animals at a place that has ever since been known as Bear Lake.

When Uncle Captain and his guests drove back to Los Angeles and Wilmington, life at Lake Vineyard settled back into temporary tranquility. These peaceful periods never lasted too long, for the Pattons were very hospitable and their doors stood open to the world. Georgie liked the quiet evenings almost as well as the exciting nights of fiesta. He and Nita would sit on the floor in the long living room, dominated by Don Benito's portrait, while his father or Aunt Annie Wilson read aloud to them. By the time he was six Georgie knew the thrilling martial verses of the *Illiad* and the adventurous *Odyssey* and many of the classic stories of olden times. He was familiar with much of the Bible and could say the Litany and the Order of Morning Prayer. He always preferred books about soldiers and battles, and when his aunt tired and stopped to rest, he would say imperiously, "Read, Aunt Nannie, read!"

Quite often his father's close friend, Colonel John Moseby, the great Confederate cavalry leader, would drop in for dinner. Then Georgie would be enthralled by true stories of the days when the quiet old gentleman and his friend General J. E. B. Stuart were the terror of the Union armies in Virginia.

Georgie's paternal grandfather, the first General George Smith Patton, had served in the Confederate Amy all through the war, until he was killed leading his men at the disastrous battle of Cedar Creek. Another Patton brother had been killed at Gettysburg and the remaining two were badly wounded. The Pattons, like the Wilsons, were fighting men.

Georgie's father was an exception. Although he had been educated, in the family tradition, at the Virginia Military Institute, he was a gentle, scholarly man whose delicate health predisposed him to love books more than the rough-and-tumble of active life. He had come to California from Charleston, West Virginia, with his widowed mother soon after the War Between the States, and here he had fallen in love with the daughter of rampageous old Don Benito Wilson. They were married in the little Church of Our Savior, at San Gabriel, which was built of bricks fired at Lake Vineyard, and there Georgie was christened soon after his birth in 1885. To that same church General George Smith Patton, Jr., returned in 1945 to give thanks for victory.

CHAPTER 2

AN EMBRYONIC GENERAL

WHEN GEORGIE PATTON WAS TEN YEARS OLD, HE made up his mind. By that time he had a surprising knowledge of military history, though he had, rather astonishingly, not yet learned to read—for two reasons: first, that there was no good school near the ranch; second, it seemed hardly worth the trouble to him, since Father, Mother, and Aunt Nannie read all the books he wanted to hear.

Georgie remembered virtually every word they read, and he liked to act out the historic events. Nita was his partner and his stooge. She was Hector slain beneath the walls of Troy, and Brutus falling on his sword; Antony fleeing from Actium, and Napoleon surrendering to the British. Georgie was always victorious, and his battles were not just play to him.

One day he announced quietly, "I'm going to be a great general and make history."

He wasn't bragging; he was simply stating a fact.

Patton, boy and man, had a one-track mind. The track had many spurs and loops, but the main line ran straight to its ultimate objective. Unless one knew the intense—at times terrible—determination of the man, it would be hard to believe that a boy of ten could choose a course and pursue it as relentlessly as did Georgie. From the moment he announced his ambition to become a general, he consciously shaped his work, and even his play, to that end.

He was a thin, delicate-looking child, but he set himself a course of exercise that developed surprising strength in his arms and legs and hardened his body.

Georgie and his great friend Charlie Nordhoff, who later was a coauthor of *Mutiny on the Bounty*, liked to camp out in the ravine behind the house. One night they heard a horrifying crashing in the dense undergrowth.

"It's a bear!" whispered Charlie.

"Yes, I think so," said Georgie in a trembling voice.

"Come on, let's make a run for the house," Charlie suggested.

"No, we can't."

"Why not?"

"Good generals don't run away," said Georgie.

Two shaky, tired little boys came back to the house next morning, but Georgie had defied that nonexistent bear.

One day, when Georgie was twelve, Mr. Patton, strolling through the garden, came upon his son and Georgie's faithful enemy, Nita, playing with toy soldiers. As the scholarly older man studied the scene of combat, something vaguely familiar struck him.

"Why, that looks like Gettysburg!" he said.

"It is," said Georgie. "Here's Seminary Ridge. Lee and his staff are there, and off to the right is Longstreet's Corps. See he's just ordering Pickett's Brigade forward. Now across the path is Little Round Top, and those are Sickles' men in the tall grass—the wheat field of course."

"Where's Big Round Top?" asked Mr. Patton.

Georgie's face fell. "I guess I forgot it," he admitted. "I'll make it now."

Georgie had actually built a reasonably good model of the terrain of Gettysburg before putting out his soldiers. He continued to play with them until he went to Virginia Military Institute at the age of seventeen, setting up all the great battles of history, complete with increasingly exact topographical models of the terrain.

Nita took part in George's preparation for a military life, usually willingly—but sometimes distressedly, as on the day she found the dead frog. With a womanly reaction—rare for her—she cried out, and Georgie came running up.

"What is it?"

"A dead frog," Nita answered, "awfully dead!"

Georgie exhumed the corpse with a long stick, so that it lay in full view on the grass. "Soldiers must be able to look on the face of death unmoved," he said sententiously.

"I can't! Can you?" Nita observed.

"Not quite," Georgie admitted. "We've got to harden ourselves." He plucked two ripe oranges from a tree. "We'll eat these while looking at the frog."

"I don't want an orange, and I don't want to look at that frog!" Nita wailed.

"Do you want to be a sissy all your life? Eat that orange!" her brother said sternly.

With their eyes resolutely fixed on the disintegrating remains, the two children ate their oranges. It was fortunate, indeed, for Nita that no fox cubs were available at Lake Vineyard, else she might have found herself in the role of the Spartan boy who stoically allowed the cub he had concealed beneath his cloak to gnaw his vitals.

Peach Blossom, a fat and amiable Shetland pony, also enacted many roles, from Alexander's Bucephalus to General Lee's gray charger, Traveler. She was Georgie's first horse; and when she wasn't carrying famous generals across country, she was breeding a race of rugged little ponies, half Shetland and half horse, on which Georgie later mounted himself and his friends. On these same ponies Patton, on leave from West Point in 1907, taught his friends the game of polo in the alfalfa field below the ranch.

It was a foregone conclusion that Patton would be a cavalryman and he practiced for the part in his own special way.

Mounted on his big charger, Lord Marmion, fifteen-year-old George S. Patton, Jr., chief scout of an imaginary army, rode northward across the desert plain. The reins hung loose on his horse's neck while he studied a topographical survey map of the San Gabriel Valley, on which he constantly made notes for the information of his fictitious commander-in-chief. He had been riding since early morning, and the sun was now so low in the west that the moving shadow of horse and boy was elongated until it might have been the silhouette of Cervantes' Knight and his gaunt charger, Rosinante.

When the sun finally dropped behind the western hills and the plain was lighted only by the reflected splendor of the Sierra peaks, Georgie prepared to camp. Ignoring the occasional lights that suggested human habitation, he chose a small canyon. He loosened the precisely packed blanket roll and stripped Lord Marmion of the English saddle, which he always used in preference to the convenient Western type because it more closely approximated a cavalryman's outfit. He watered and fed his horse, then ate his own rations cold because a fire might disclose his presence to the "enemy." As the clammy California cold poured with the night into the valley, he wrapped himself in a blanket and lay down to sleep soundly on the desert floor.

In the morning Georgie treated himself to a hot breakfast cooked over a fire built so carefully that there was no trace of smoke, and then got under way. All day he rode, carefully noting every feature of the country and planning the movements of his army accordingly.

Toward afternoon he approached the end of his mission. Before reaching it, he washed in a mountain stream, changed to fine whipcord riding breeches and a handsome silk shirt, and combed his yellow hair into shining order.

These elaborate preparations were due to the fact that the ultimate objective of Georgie's arduous scouting was the home of a fair young lady in the Puente Hills, which is also typical of a good cavalryman, as any study of history will show.

Georgie's formal education began at the age of twelve, when he entered Doctor S. C. Clark's school for boys in Pasadena. Among young Patton's schoolmates were Charlie Nordhoff, Frank Graves and the Phillips boys.

It took Georgie only a year and a half to make up all the studies he had lost. He was never a great student—except in regard to things which interested him; namely, anything that a general might need to know—but he could study with tremendous concentration when he had to.

Going to school did not interfere too much with young Patton's rugged outdoor life. There were always Lord Marmion and Sir Galahad waiting to be exercised when he got home from school; if there was not time then, he'd rise before dawn for an early gallop across country.

On weekends Georgie often took long hikes with this friend Doctor Holden, the famous naturalist, who taught him about the flowers and plants and animals of the country. This knowledge, too, Georgie stored up for possible use in war.

In the summertime the Pattons usually went to their cottage on Catalina, the superb, rocky island off the California coast, which is often compared with the Isle of Capri. At that time Joseph, William, and Hancock Banning and Mr. Patton owned Catalina. They had built the Hotel Metropole, a vast, ramshackle firetrap surrounded by cottages for summer visitors. There was also a tent city where Angelenos could rent a tent for a small sum and enjoy the outdoor life in the perfect summer climate.

In the wild interior of the island the Bannings and Mr. Patton had a big ranch run by a family of Mexicans. Here they kept riding horses, and raised food for their business enterprises on the coast.

Joseph and Hancock Banning managed the Metropole, and seafaring Captain William had the steamers that plied between the island and the mainland. The Pattons lived in a cottage but ate at the hotel, since Mr. Patton liked to keep his finger on the pulse of his affairs.

On Catalina, Georgie learned to sail by a process of trial and error. Mr. Patton bought him a small sloop, and one afternoon father and son set sail together in the *Elaine*. Neither of them knew a boom from a bowsprit, so they tried to copy what other boats were doing.

They were fairly successful up to the point when Georgie asked, "Why do all the boats turn toward the wind?"

"I don't know," Mr. Patton admitted. "Try turning the other way and see what happens."

Georgie pulled the tiller toward him. The *Elaine* slowly

swung away from the wind, heeling hard. Suddenly she sprang upright like a released spring. The boom swung over, taking Mr. Patton's hat with it, there was a crashing jerk and the little sloop went down on her side, with water pouring over the gunwale. By a seeming miracle she righted, and lay water-logged and shaking like a frightened horse.

Mr. Patton looked regretfully after his fine straw hat. "That must be why," he said.

On Catalina, Georgie first learned the joys of hunting. The island was infested with wild goats, which bounded over its crags and dales with all the abandon of bighorns in the Rockies and were just as much fun to hunt. At first he was allowed to go with the men only to watch the sport, but when he was eleven his father gave him a one-shot .22. When he was sure that Georgie knew how to use it safely, Mr. Patton turned his son loose.

Georgie hunted goats early and late and between times practiced on targets until he became a crack shot. He took care of the cheap little gun as though it were a thousand-dollar fowling piece—it now belongs to his son. All his life Georgie loved weapons. The feel of them in his hands was more delicious to him than is the touch of fine jade to a Chinese mandarin. He eventually became proficient with all types of firearms from a diminutive .22 automatic to an antiaircraft cannon, but the type he liked best was the traditional—and obsolete—Western six-gun. Even in his choice of weapons Georgie was an incurable romantic.

CHAPTER 3

FOR ALWAYS

BEATRICE BANNING AYER LIVED IN A GRAY STONE house on Commonwealth Avenue in the city of Boston. In summer the Ayers moved to a big Italianate villa on the harbor at Pride's Crossing, which is the very center of those correct and affluent colonies on the North Shore of Massachusetts Bay. But they were far from being the stuffy sort of family one might suppose. They lived in great, formal houses in a completely informal way.

For one thing, Bea Ayer had four half-brothers and sisters and a younger brother and sister of her own—seven Ayer children in all. When her father built the house at Pride's Crossing, he said to his architect, "I want a room for all the family to gather in—so big that any of them can study, or read or write letters or play games without disturbing the others."

It was an immense room, running the whole length of the central portion of the house, with long windows that looked across the bay to Beverly and the long wharf at Salem, to which the clipper ships used to come home from all the oceans of the world. The rest of the house was on the same scale and, big as it was, it was always chock-full of people, for the Ayers are a hospitable breed. Mr. Ayer named his home Avalon, thinking of Tennyson's words:

> ... *Avilion*
> *Where falls not hail or rain or any snow*
> *Nor ever wind blows loudly ...*

In the summer of 1902, when Bea Ayer was sixteen, Mr. Ayer decided to take his family to California to visit their Banning cousins. Bea found Catalina very exciting—it was the first time since she had been grown up that she had stayed at a summer resort. She liked the big hotel with its high-ceilinged bedrooms, and its big verandas that were always full of people. The Saturday night hops were great fun—and so were the expeditions to the Mexican ranch in the interior, and the rides up the mountain trails with their sudden astonishingly beautiful views across the blue channel to the hills and mountains of the mainland.

Most exciting of all was her cousin-by-courtesy Georgie Patton. He was a tall, thin boy of seventeen, with gray eyes that sometimes looked green, a big, straight nose, a fair, florid complexion; and yellow-gold hair. Georgie never seemed to have time for all the things he wanted to do. He rushed from one place to another as though he were possessed by a busy little demon. He talked with tremendous enthusiasm in a high-pitched voice, and some of the things he said were very funny indeed; for he loved to make jokes about everybody, including himself.

Bea went everywhere she could with him, and he seemed to like having her along. Even when they were just out for a stroll along the cliffs, he walked so fast that she had to trot to keep up with him; but she didn't mind that at all.

After the Ayers had been on the island a couple of weeks, Mrs. Patton proposed an expedition to Lake Vineyard. Bea was delighted at the prospect of seeing the famous ranch, though her pleasure was somewhat dimmed when Georgie announced that he was too busy to go. They drove over in one of Captain William's Concord coaches; even with six horses it took nearly all day to make the thirty miles.

Bea loved the long adobe ranch house with its pleasant informality and its great cavernous cellars where the wine was stored. She found that the Pattons lived even more casually than the Ayers.

For example, as she walked down the corridor with Mrs. Patton one afternoon, she saw a small, furry creature who popped into a hole in the wall as they approached. What was that, Aunt Ruth?" she asked.

Mrs. Patton's answer made her jump. "It must have been one of the skunks."

"Skunks!"

Her aunt laughed. "A family of them has lived in the attic for generations. Would you like to see them?"

"I guess so," said Bea dubiously.

Mrs. Patton piloted her up a flight of ladder-like stairs to an enormous, gloomy attic that ran the full length of the house. There was just light enough to make out the litter of old furniture and the big casks of olives that filled it. From dim corners and recesses Bea saw dozens of bright little eyes staring at her.

When she was safely downstairs again, she asked the question that had been boiling inside of her. "Don't your little skunks ever get—noisome?"

"I guess they like us too much. They are very useful, for they keep the house free of rats. In all these years they have misbehaved but once."

"When was that?"

"Ask Uncle George," said her aunt, smiling. "He loves to tell the story."

Mr. Patton told the tale with relish. It seemed that years before, when he was courting his wife, he had a very serious rival, a musical young man who used to bring Ruth Wilson all the newest songs and sit beside her while she played and they sang together. Patton, who was tone-deaf and hated music, could do nothing but sit and glower, fearing the worst.

Mr. Patton ended the tale with a flourish. "One lucky day," he said, "one of the skunks attacked that fancy young fellow and, while they were burning his clothes, I married the girl. So long as I live, those skunks will have a good home!"

Back on Catalina, Bea knew that she was in love with Georgie and he with her. They never spoke of it, for those two never needed to discuss important things. Their minds and emotions so blended that they seemed to understand each other without words.

Georgie had made up his mind to go to West Point, probably in 1904. That meant it would be at least six years before they could be married—six years in which they would see each other for but the briefest moments; six years in which Georgie would be concentrating his tremendous energy on the business of preparing himself to be a soldier. In fact, he was already so wrapped in his career and so sure of its outcome that Bea's mother dubbed him "General" and always called him by that name.

Bea was a very pretty girl, small and beautifully built, with large blue eyes, soft brown hair, and a lovely peaches-and-cream complexion. She would have many beaux, some with great names and wealth. It seemed extremely foolish to give her heart to so young a man, with such distant prospects. But she could not help it, nor did she want to. Neither did the thought of those long years trouble her; she knew that she could wait for their fulfillment. She was happy to be Georgie's girl—then and always.

CHAPTER 4

THE SACRED PLAIN

MANY A BOY STANDING FOR THE FIRST TIME ON THE imposing stretch of bright green turf, surrounded by the turreted towers of West Point, feels mightily oppressed by the harsh constrictions of discipline and the anonymity of the gray-clad ranks. Not so Georgie Patton. Even at the beginning, when he was but a "beast" (a repulsive creature alleged to have crawled out of a sewer, and the butt of every cadet who had been at the Academy a year or more), he felt the exaltation, the ease of being in his rightful place. This was the straight path to his goal; the Sacred Plain trodden by the men he meant to emulate, or surpass.

Georgie went to West Point in June, 1904, having won his appointment through a competitive examination held by

Senator T. G. Bard of California. The preceding winter he had spent in preparation at the Virginia Military Institute, his father's Alma Mater.

At V.M.I., Georgie was not popular, and at West Point he was cordially disliked by many of the cadets, though he made a few lifelong friends. That was because he was both insufferably cocky and intensely serious about soldiering. He was cocky because he felt himself to be a better soldier, by temperament and preparation, than his classmates. On the day he arrived at the Academy he knew more of military history than many of them would ever learn. Also, he had familiarized himself with a thousand trivia of West Point custom, such as how to make his bed, where to hang his clothes, and what to answer when an upperclassman asked, "Whom does a plebe rank?" (The answer is: "The Supe's dog, the Commandant's cat, and all the admirals in the whole durn Navy.")

You might suppose that his familiarity with regulations and his military bearing would have smoothed Georgie's path. On the contrary, it seemed to infuriate the upper classmen. He knew too darned much, and they rode him unmercifully for it. Georgie took the hazing in good part—he even felt a sort of Spartan pleasure in it—for it was right in line with his theory of how to toughen a soldier.

At the end of his plebe year Georgie received the first of the staggering blows that he met and survived in the course of his controversial military career. When the results of the final examinations were posted, he saw that the irregularity of his early schooling had caught up with him; he had failed in math. It might have meant dismissal, but instead he was dropped a class.

So he began all over again, a lowly plebe ranked by everyone but a dog and cat. The classmates he had expected to outshine, he must now address as "Sir." Most serious of all, he had lost nearly a hundred points in the sacred seniority rating of the Army. The general's stars on which his eyes were fixed receded several light years in his firmament.

Whatever has been said against Patton—and plenty it is—no one ever suggested that he couldn't take it. His demotion neither embittered him nor chastened him—it was a reverse, not a defeat. His confidence in his future was unshaken, and his behavior was more insufferably cocky than ever.

Patton's unpopularity began to rise when he was a yearling. He was what is known as a "make"; that is, he was out to achieve rank and honors at the Academy as well as in his later career. He went at it—as he did everything else—all out. He had no time for fooling, and no respect for persons; Georgie was on his way.

Nor was this all. He had a peculiar notion that regulations were meant to be obeyed. His idea was not shared by his fellows, who regarded them as rules to be evaded if possible. To them the unwritten laws were much more important; and one of the most sacred of these is that a man may not report his classmate for breaking the rules, even though it is his duty to do so. Georgie took a different view.

At summer camp, when he was a yearling, he caught a classmate *in flagrante delicto.*

"Are you going to skin [report] me?" the boy asked.

"Certainly," Georgie replied.

That evening eight unpleasantly large young men paid a business call on Georgie.

"Were you serious when you said you were going to skin Tommy?" the leader asked.

"I'm always serious about military matters," Patton replied.

"Military mucilage!" said the other. "If you make that report, we'll beat you within an inch of your life."

"Tommy's name is going in the Skin Book," Georgie said. "I'll fight you now, one at a time, and when I get out of the hospital I'll start again where I left off."

They didn't take him up on the proposal. Neither did they love him for it.

By the summer of his second-class year Georgie's insistence on the rigid enforcement of discipline had become a very sore point indeed, as it was, later, in the armies he commanded. The cadets at West Point, like the men of Seventh and Third Armies, thought it was merely his way of asserting himself. But it was, in fact, a cardinal principle of the military philosophy he was already developing. As he said to his cousin Joe Banning in later years, "An undisciplined army always has the greatest casualties. A general who disciplines his troops until he gets spontaneous, automatic reaction to his commands will have the lowest rate of casualties."

His classmates called him "Quill [i.e., drip] Georgie," and their sneering comment in the Furlough Book of 1907 stated that his desire was "to get back, so as to be near that dear old Skin Book." Beneath that remark they bitterly recorded the verse:

> *He stands erect;*
> *Right Martial is his air,*
> *His form and movements.*

All that didn't stop Georgie from doing his duty as he saw it, and in his last year he risked the anger of the entire corps. It was the custom of the cadets to treat unpopular officers to the "silence." When the offending officer entered a room, the cadets would spring to attention and stand in absolute silence until he left. It was an expression of profound contempt under the guise of respect. George considered that it bordered on mutiny.

Once, when Georgie was commanding a battalion, he marched his cadets in to lunch. The great mess hall was filled with men standing at their places by the tables, waiting for the command "Seats!" An unpopular lieutenant entered the room, and Georgie felt the cadets stiffening to give him the silence. In a voice that rang shrilly through the vaulted hall, he commanded, "Battalion! Attention!"

The amazed cadets stiffened to rigidity.

"Right face!"

The men swung sharply, facing the door.

"Forward march!"

In automatic reaction to the command, the lines of cadets moved forward; formed into squads; and marched, empty-bellied, out of the hall!

Georgie went in for athletics as violently as for soldiering. He played football with such reckless abandon that he never made the team, since each year he broke one or more bones in practice scrimmages. He became a superb horseman and began to play polo, the game he came to love best. He was one of the best swordsmen at the Academy, and an expert rifleman with an A for breaking a long-standing record at the butts. But he won his highest honors at track. In his second-class year he tied the intercollegiate record for the 220 low hurdles, and the following year he broke his own record.

On a certain occasion Georgie's speed afoot was put to a weird test. One evening he and Cadet Joseph Carberry, who held the Academy record for the 100-yard dash, decided to go A.W.O.L. to the neighboring town of Highland Falls to get an ice-cream soda. They had slipped safely past the guard, on their return, and thought themselves safe when they saw the figure of an officer running after them.

"Come on, Joe! He can't catch us," Georgie said.

They put on a terrific burst of speed, but as soon as they slackened pace, they sensed their pursuer behind them. Again they dashed ahead, and ran until they were out of breath. The moment they eased off, the relentless tracker was upon them. Try as they would, they could not shake that shadowy figure— who never closed with them, yet hovered, ghostlike, on their trail. Their fear of being caught turned to a sort of panic. They reached their quarters with bursting lungs and laboring hearts, to fling themselves, fully dressed, into bed.

The mystery was solved the following morning when they received an order to report to young Captain Joseph R. Stillwell. At the Academy a few years before, Stillwell had been the crack miler.

"He'll throw the book at us," Carberry opined as they marched to Stillwell's office.

"He'll be quite justified," and Georgie glumly.

But when they stood at rigid attention before his desk, all Vinegar Joe said, in his acidulous voice, was, "Mr. Carberry, Mr. Patton, permit me to give you a piece of advice—never go out for the distances. That will be all, gentlemen!"

From his position just in front of the cadet major, George Patton faced the regiment drawn up for the last parade of the class of 1909. The long, straight line of men was a brilliant spectacle—shining kepis, gray coats with gleaming cross belts and bright buttons, knife-edged white trousers in exact alignment, scarlet guerdons marking their companies—as they stood in utter silence awaiting the final commands.

Georgie wheeled to face the cadet major, received his orders and again about-faced. In his uniform of cadet adjutant, with gold chevrons on his sleeves, scarlet sash, and tall plumed helmet, holding the polished sword in his hand, he was the most resplendent of all that gaudy company. As he filled his lungs he seemed to grow even taller, and his high voice carried across the Plain with a piercing urgency of command.

In swift, precise obedience the line of cadets stiffened to attention; five hundred bayonets flashed as rifles came up to the shoulders. The Hell Cats (fife and drum corps) began to play and, company by company, the regiment swung into platoon front, and began to march past.

As Georgie stood rigidly with the small group of ranking cadet officers, watching the beautiful unison of moving legs and swinging arms, and the exact slope of the bayoneted rifles, his heart was turbulent with emotion. To his wildly romantic nature this was an apogee of life, a moment of high fulfillment; the end of one wonderful time of preparation, the beginning of another. The night before, he had prayed passionately in the chapel, like a squire on the eve of knighthood, that God would give him the strength and wisdom and courage to be a good solider. Now he stood confident in his purpose.

To the spectators his face betrayed nothing of the wild turbulence within him. It looked as coldly arrogant as the sculpture of a battle monument; the lips were a thin harsh line, the eyes an adamantine gray. Then the colors came by for the last time—the gold-fringed, emblazoned banner of the regiment and the rippling, vivid beauty of the Stars and Stripes, streaming from its polished staff.

Cadet Adjutant Patton's face crumpled like a little boy's, and his tears fell uncontrolled.

CHAPTER 5

CAVALRY POST

BEA AYER HAD WAITED RESOLUTELY. THROUGH ALL the excitement of her debut—made in the grand manner of those pre-World War I days—of trips abroad, of beaux who languished—as was fashionable—for a kind look, she had been completely steadfast. And Georgie had never looked at another girl.

Bea had come to all the hops at West Point, and Georgie had spent most of his brief leaves in Boston and Pride's Crossing. Of course Bea was on hand to pin the golden bars on his shoulder straps.

Soon afterward he formally proposed—it would not have been correct to do so before graduation. Bea accepted forthrightly, with some indication of relief.

"But you must have known I would propose the moment I had anything to offer you," he said.

"Of course I did," she answered. "Still you never know what you'll get till the orders are posted."

After a little she asked, "When can we be married?"

"We'll have to wait a year," said Georgie sternly. "I can't take on a career and a wife at the same time and do justice to either."

Patton inevitably chose the cavalry, and was assigned to Troop K, 15th Cavalry, stationed at Fort Sheridan, Illinois. The small and dusty army post would have seemed dull to most young officers, but to Patton it was a place of excitement and accomplishment. His enthusiasm was spurred by his good fortune in finding Troop K under the command of a splendid officer.

Captain Frank A. Marshall had been an instructor at West Point. When he left, he said to Georgie, "If you choose the cavalry, I will ask for you." Even then he sensed the potential greatness in the eager and rambunctious young lieutenant.

In return Georgie gave Marshall all the love and loyalty of a generous heart. He respected his senior enormously, and eagerly accepted the guidance Marshall freely offered. Their relationship was a little like that of father and son, and it remained so until the death of Brigadier General Marshall in an airplane accident in 1921.

This was the first of a series of close friendships that Patton formed with older officers of the Army. Others who were very dear to him were Generals Pershing, Guy V. Henry; James D. Harbord; Charles P. Summerall, who had also instructed Georgie as a cadet, and George Simons, who contributed a piece of wisdom that was to become part of Patton's creed. On one occasion Georgie had a choice of three posts. He wrote to Simons asking which he should accept. Simons' reply was, "There is only one criterion in choosing between jobs, what will help your country most."

On May 26, 1910, nearly eight years from the day they met, Georgia and Bea Ayer were married in the Episcopal Church of St. John at Beverly Farms, Massachusetts. There was a big reception at Avalon, with guests filling the great drawing room and spilling out onto the terrace above the bay.

Georgie and Bea had their picture taken there, against the granite balustrade. It shows her in her mother's satin wedding dress with a flowing lace overskirt draped up and back to suggest a bustle. Bea is grinning with delight, but Georgie wears his military face. Very young and stern he looks in his gorgeous dress uniform—on his breast the badge of an expert rifleman, the lonely precursor of all those glittering medals and ribbons and orders he was yet to win.

After a brief honeymoon Georgie took his bride to Fort Sheridan. It was quite a change from Avalon. As the youngest officer of the post, Patton rated half of a small double house.

When she saw it, Bea was a little dismayed. "I didn't know anybody lived in two-family houses," she said.

"We do, for a long time," remarked Georgie.

"I don't really mind," Bea said quickly—and she didn't. "But," she added, "let's not dress for dinner tonight; it seems sort of foolish here."

"The poorer your surroundings, the more important it is to keep up your standards," Georgie said. "We'll dress for dinner."

Bea got her introduction to army life early the next morning. She found an official order slipped under the door. It read:

The sun will rise at 6:45 A.M. and set at 7:23 P.M.
By order of
COLONEL PITCHER, *Commanding*

The usual misadventures of the newly married couple were complicated, in Bea's case, by her ignorance of the rigid punctilio of an army post. Even Georgie was not always able to enlighten her. For example, on one occasion the Post was thrown into a flurry by the arrival of the Inspectors General.

"What do they inspect?" asked Bea.

"I'm not sure," Georgie admitted. "Better get the house shipshape."

Bea spent a frantic day housecleaning; toward evening she had a collection of odds and ends, including her husband's favorite old shooting jacket. In desperation she slammed them all into the hall closet, locked it, and, to make sure it could not be opened, threw the key into the shrubbery.

When her husband came home, she asked, "When are the I.G.'s coming?"

"They left long ago," said Patton. "Say, where's that old shooting coat of mine?"

"Oh, Georgie . . ."

Later that evening the Post was treated to the remarkable sight of Lieutenant and Mrs. George S. Patton, Jr., crawling on their hands and knees through the shrubbery, nosing the ground like a couple of hounds looking for a buried bone.

Bea soon picked up the ways of army life, and became a great asset to her husband. Her command of French enabled her to help him translate the textbooks used by *L'Ecole de Cavalerie*, of France; these official translations enhanced his reputation. She was always ready to assist with his projects for improving the post, one of which set an Army precedent.

Patton was disturbed by the fact that enlisted men at Fort Sheridan had no recreation other than beer swilling and pool playing in the neighboring town. He organized a football team, for which he and his wife bought the uniforms and equipment. Georgie played on the team himself, while Bea acted as cheer leader and drummed up a gallery for the home games.

This was the first enlisted man's team in the Army.

Meanwhile Georgie was learning to play really good polo. He joined the Onwentsia Club, where he met some of the best players in the Midwest, and in his usual thoroughgoing way practiced long and hard. Of course Bea was at all the games to cheer him on.

In fact, Bea so identified herself with her husband's life that she became an integral part of it, sharing all his pleasures and problems and, indeed, his very thoughts. When they were first married, she felt herself barred from one aspect of him. Patton was extremely religious. He prayed night and morning, and before every special occasion. Bea had been brought up as a good churchwoman, but she did not feel the need for constant, intimate contact with God. She watched her husband and wondered.

One afternoon she came into the room to find Georgie, dressed for polo, on his knees before the bed. His helmet hung on the bedpost, his mallet was leaning against the wall, and his polished boots stuck out behind him with the naked spurs upturned.

Bea felt an irresistible compulsion to understand. "Georgie," she said, "I've simply got to know about all this praying. For instance, what are you praying for now—to win the game?"

Georgie swiveled around on his marrowbones. "Hell, no!" he said. "I'm praying to do my best."

Two of Patton's cousins had joined the ministry and he himself thought of it seriously. He wanted desperately to be a soldier, but he knew that, if the call to serve the Church came to him, he would have to obey his heavenly Commander-in-Chief. So he prayed that he would not get the call.

Mrs. Ayer had given her daughter a piece of Polonian advice when she began her army life: "Make friends with everyone; confide in no one."

Bea took it so to heart that she became the enigma of Fort Sheridan. After she had been there for perhaps six months, the wife of an elderly major paid her a visit.

After talking trivialities for some time, the older woman said,

"I am the oldest lady on the post, and the others have deputed me to ask you a rather delicate question. Believe me, it is done in kindness."

"I'm sure it is," said Bea, "and I'll be glad to answer if I can."

"You have confided in no one," said her visitor, blushing a little. "We wondered if you know you are going to have a baby."

Beatrice Ayer Patton, Jr., came into the world as befitted her father's daughter. It was late on an afternoon in March, 1911. On the parade ground, outside the bedroom window, the troop was mustering for the solemn ceremony of retreat. Bandsmen raised their polished instruments to their lips; a gunner twitched his lanyard . . . and little Bea's first shrill cry mingled with the strains of "The Star-Spangled Banner" and the crash of the sunset gun.

CHAPTER 6

THE FIFTH OLYMPIAD

FORT MYER, IN 1912, WAS A VERY DIFFERENT PLACE from Sheridan. Even the red brick Army houses looked pretty and homelike set among its ancient trees and lovely soft green turf. Just beyond the blue river lay Washington, basking in the last days of tranquility; over which the engaging rotundity of President William Howard Taft seemed to cast a benevolent glow.

The long, long peace had been interrupted only by little wars, and the minds of men had begun to accept the idea that peace, not war, was the natural condition of the world. Indeed, what with The Hague Court and the apparently growing sense of unity among peoples, most Americans believed that there would never be another big war.

Lulled by this semblance of serenity, many young officers took life easy. But Patton hustled as though the outbreak of hostilities were a matter of minutes. He paid little attention to Washington society, concentrating, instead, on his work at the Fort. Besides his regular military duties and his constant study to improve himself, he organized polo teams and horse shows to keep the officers awake and doing, and got up riding classes for the enlisted men. Thus he became an outstanding figure among the younger officers, despite the fact that he had nearly got off to a very bad start.

This occurred because Georgie hated answering the telephone and was always telling Bea to make excuses for him. On their very first day at Fort Myer, Patton was lying on a sofa when the telephone rang.

Bea answered it and called, "For you, Georgie."

"Tell them that I've just had a stroke of paralysis," he replied.

Bea gravely said, "Mr. Patton says to tell you that he has just had a stroke of paralysis." Then she remarked demurely to her husband, "That was the commanding officer."

Georgie shot off the sofa and dashed for the telephone. No one knows whether the blue smoke in the room was caused by the speed of his passage or by the violence of his language.

During his tour at Fort Myer, Georgie became aide to

General Leonard Wood and, also, a great friend of a man who, unforeseeably, was to become an agent of his destiny. President Taft's Secretary of War, Henry L. Stimson, often came to ride at the fort. It pleased him to have as a companion a young officer who was so knowledgeable and keen about his profession. The friendship lasted through all the years until, under wildly improbable circumstances, Stimson again became Secretary of War.

The flags of fifty nations flew from the staffs along the top of the new stadium in Stockholm. The black eagle of Hohenzollern Germany spread its wings benignly beside the tricolor of France; and the elaborate banner of the Tsars rippled peacefully near the Union Jack, while the Stars and Stripes flew gaily as a symbol of America's first participation with the nations of the world in the friendly combat of the Olympic Games. None of the thousands of spectators, banked up to the eaves of the great concrete stands, could know that it was the last time all those flags would fly together in amity.

Georgie Patton, in the pistol butts on the turfed floor of the arena, was terribly conscious of his responsibility as America's representative before the eyes of the world—too conscious. He had been chosen to represent America in the Modern

Pentathlon, a series of five contests which included pistol shooting, swimming, cross-country riding, a distance run, and swordsmanship. The Pentathlon might have been designed to suit his warlike taste, and he was determined to do or die.

From the moment of his selection, with its unique opportunity to gain glory in a world at peace, Georgie had trained like a madman. It seemed to Bea that he never stopped practicing from morning till night, and he thought about it all night long. So hard had he worked that in three months his weight had dropped from 190 pounds to 150 pounds. With his six feet plus of height, it was far too little—he looked like a medieval ascetic, all skin and bones and blazing spirit.

The long strain had worn his temper thin, and stretched his nerves like wire stays. The three women who loved him best— Bea and Nita and his mother—watched with a kind of anguish as he took his place before the movable target. Yesterday, in practice, he had broken the world's record: 98 points out of a possible 100. But . . .

The man-shaped target leaped up before Georgie's eyes, and he began to shoot. At once he knew that this was not like yesterday. The sure coordination was lacking; he had to force his muscles to obey. He forced them well—45 points out of a possible 50, in that first round—but he had not done his best.

Bitterly blaming himself, he came up for the second round and was destroyed by his own ardor. He missed the target twice and scored but 30 points. His final score was 150 out of 200, which left him well down the list in the contest that was his best chance of all. The Stockholm afternoon paper gallantly said that the judges must have miscounted the score.

The next day was the swimming. In the dressing rooms before the event Gustave Wersäl, of the Swedish team, came up to Patton carrying a photo album.

"Let me show you some pictures of my house," he said. "It is very beautiful."

Holding a tight rein on his jumping nerves, in the cause of civility, Patton replied, "I can't look at them now. I'm going into the tank in a few minutes."

The fine Swedish sportsman smiled compassionately. "If I had had my album to show you yesterday," he said, "you would have beaten me."

The story of Patton's effort in the Pentathlon resembles his football record at West Point—he tried too hard. And so it was to be until, at the climax of his career, his audacity was seasoned by age and experience.

In the swimming race, sheer courage overcame lack of technique and—surprisingly—he finished second, utterly spent. In the *épée* duel, his slashing attack overcame most of his opponents; but some of the experienced Europeans were too wily for him. The cross-country ride found him on a borrowed Swedish horse, with which he finished fourth—the first three being Swedes, who knew the terrain.

The final event was the 2.5 mile run. Patton was off like a whippet and ran, through the hot summer noon, almost at full stretch all the way. He led to within 50 yards of the finish, where Asbrink, of Sweden, passed him. Patton crossed the line in second place and fell in a dead faint in front of the King's box.

The sole American to finish in the Pentathlon placed fourth among 47 contestants, a most respectable showing. But Patton never wished to be respectable—he wanted to win. However, the bitterness of defeat was assuaged by the knowledge that in all but one event he had done his best.

Besides, he made some fine new friends. The Swedish athletes loved him for his blazing spirit and his dash. He seemed to them to embody the virtues of America, and perhaps its youthful fault of impetuosity. They long remembered him, and most of them, including Gustave Wersäl, were on hand to make merry with him the next time he came to Stockholm— in 1945, when he had just won the greatest cross-country obstacle race in the annals of the world.

CHAPTER 7

THE BRIGHT FLASH
OF WAR

ALL THE ROMANTICISM OF PATTON'S NATURE
demanded that he excel in swordsmanship, and at Stockholm
he decided he was not good enough. So he took Bea to Saumur,
in France, and studied fencing at *L' École de Cavalerie*. When he
returned to Fort Myer he lectured and wrote on the French use
of the saber, and described the American cavalry weapon as an
"unintelligent copy of an Oriental scimitar." The military
authorities were so impressed that they commissioned him to
design a new saber, which became the standard weapon of the
U.S. Cavalry. Thus he got his first nickname: "Saber George."
They also sent him back to Saumur the following summer, 1913,
for further study.

In the course of this trip Georgie and Bea scouted the Bocage country of Normandy on foot, because Patton thought he might have to fight there someday. Looking at the little fields enclosed by the almost impassable hedgerows, Bea thought that it would be impossible for an army to break a resolute defense.

"Most things seem impossible until they are done," said her husband. "It was impossible to take elephants over the Alpine passes, but Hannibal did it. If necessary, I can fight my way through the Bocage."

Patton's next assignment was to the great cavalry post, Fort Riley, Kansas, both as Master of the Sword and as a student in the Mounted Service School. While he was there, the unthinkable happened. Almost casually the long peace was broken at last and, in their terrible ignorance, the enormous conscript armies of Europe marched gaily off to war. German Uhlans clashed with French dragoons in preliminary light opera skirmishes that foretold little of modern war. Then came the first great tragic battles; Mons, where the small British army was decimated; the Marne, where Kaiser Wilhelm's monstrous war machine ground to a stop amid fearful slaughter; Tannenberg, where a little-known German general named von Hindenburg wrecked the unwieldy Russian army so completely that it never fully recovered.

Georgie Patton was beside himself. From newspaper accounts and Army reports he fought the battles step by step; it was frustrating. He wanted to be there, gaining experience, professionally, in the biggest league of all. His friend Lieutenant John Houdeman, of the French army, urged Georgie to enlist in his crack regiment of cuirassiers, mounted soldiers wearing armor, promising that he would inherit the commission of the first officer to be killed. Georgie enthusiastically had a helmet and cuirass made to order, and wrote to the War Department for "leave to go beyond the seas."

His request was turned down cold because the wiser heads in Washington were beginning to realize that, despite the official aloof attitude toward the war, the United States might need all the trained soldiers she possessed, and a lot more.

The shining helmet and cuirass, alone, remained to Georgie's romantic impulse. Mary, the Patton's Irish maid, always referred to them as "Mr. Patton's coat of arms."

The year 1915 found Patton with the 8th Cavalry at Fort Bliss, Texas. President Woodrow Wilson's peaceful intentions were being frustrated in all directions, for Mexico had become the battleground of bandit chieftains, and its relations with the United States were tense. All the available American troops were concentrated along the Border, in case of serious trouble.

Even though they should never be used, the expedition would provide training that was desperately needed because, at this time, many senior officers of the Army had never maneuvered with any force larger than a regiment.

Bea was to have another baby; and in February, 1915, she went to Lake Vineyard, where her second daughter, Ruth Ellen, was born. She was back with her husband when the lid finally blew off the Border.

The trouble came in March, 1916. Pancho Villa led a band of Mexican revolutionaries across the Border to sack the town of Columbus, New Mexico. That was too much for even President Wilson's vast patience. He called out the National Guard, and ordered Brigadier General John G. Pershing to lead a column of regulars into Mexico and capture Villa.

Fort Bliss was buzzing like a breached beehive. Everyone wanted to go on the bandit hunt, but some must be left in garrison. General Pershing lived on the Post, and everywhere he went officers and men scanned Black Jack's rugged face for an omen of their destiny. When the orders were published, the 8th Cavalry was left behind.

Georgie Patton did not give up easily. On the day the news broke he planted himself in a chair on General Pershing's porch, and sat there hour after hour. Each time the General went in or out, Patton leaped up and saluted snappily; but he never said a word. When Patton had kept his vigil for thirty-six hours, the thing became too much for Pershing's iron reserve.

"Haven't I seen you here before?" he asked.

"Yes, sir," said Patton. "I have been waiting for a chance to speak to you."

"Well, you've got it. What do you want?"

"I want to go to Mexico with you, as your aide, sir."

"I have already chosen my two aides."

"You can use a third one, sir, and if you take me I promise you will never regret it."

So, at last, Georgie Patton rode off to war in the long, clanking cavalry column that crossed the Mexican Border to chase Villa through the mountains of Chihuahua.

It was the first of many times Bea watched him go, with his face radiant in what she once described as the "bright flash of war, over almost before it begins." She understood him so well that she could almost rejoice for him, though her heart was torn. In her hand she clutched the keepsake he had given her, engraved with the word *Mizpah* meaning "The Lord watch between me and thee while we are parted one from another."

• • •

The message said: "Lieutenant Patton badly burned by exploding lamp. Being sent out in truck convoy."

Bea waited for him in the little room in Columbus, New Mexico. It was no more than a partitioned space in the loft of a warehouse marked by a sign that read: "Hay, Grain and Seed." She had given Georgie the gadgety gasoline lamp that had exploded and, of course, she blamed herself. Each afternoon she walked down the road toward the Border and waited, watching for the returning column.

She was there when it came—a cloud of dust moving across the desert, with the tops of the trucks swaying above it. The lead vehicle, a Dodge touring car, stopped at her signal, and a captain jumped out.

"This must be Mrs. Patton," he said. "Climb right in with us."

Georgie sat beside the driver with his face so swathed in dirty bandages that he looked, and smelled—like a badly preserved mummy. The captain had kept him alive for three days by feeding him bouillon through a piece of rubber tubing from a prestolite tank. Bea got in beside her husband. "I heard you were . . . recumbent," she ventured.

Through muffling bandages Georgie exploded, "Hell, no!"

He was, however, badly burned—the skin was burned off his face in patches; his ears were mere shells of cartilage.

Bea took him home to Lake Vineyard. With his mother to help nurse him, she brought him around in record time. Just thirty days after he came home, Bea saw Georgie off to war again. His fragile ears were bundled in little pongee bags.

When he was gone, Bea broke down and cried and, turning to his mother, said, "How can you see him go so cheerfully?"

Ruth Patton smiled and answered, as Bea herself learned to answer her own children, "Because it's what he wants to do. I can manage all right, if I neither look at him nor touch him."

Four men were skinning a bull in front of the small fortresslike ranch house as Lieutenant Patton and his foraging party drove up the desert trail to Rubio in two Dodge touring cars.

"I'll bet they have some corn here," Patton said. "Let's stop and see."

As the cars pulled up and the soldiers tumbled out of them, people began shooting through the narrow windows. Patton's new ivory-handled six-shooters seemed to jump from their holsters into his hands, and he emptied them at the windows before dropping on his stomach with the men. He felt almost certain that he had accidentally surprised the headquarters of General Julio Cardenas, who led the Dorados, Villa's personal bodyguard. Now he gave orders to his seven men to spread out around the ranch house.

The siege was lively while it lasted, with everybody shooting like mad and doing as little damage as though it were all being filmed in Technicolor. Throughout the action the four men went right on skinning the bull, never looking up. They evidently wanted to disassociate themselves from the whole affair.

Georgie soon began to get bored. He could, at last, say with George Washington, "I have heard the bullets whistle and there is something charming in the sound"; but he clearly was getting nowhere, and if it got dark he would lose his quarry. Suddenly he stood up and walked toward the ranch house, firing both pistols from the hips. It was the signal for action.

Three horsemen galloped around the corner of the house and rode hard toward the gate. Patton swung, shooting. He winged one, and brought the horse of another crashing down. The wounded man dashed back into the house. Patton exultantly recognized him as Cardenas. He waited while the second bandit struggled free from his dead horse; then, as the fellow stood up and fired, Patton drilled him through the heart—he was shooting better than he had at Stockholm.

The spirit seemed to have gone out of the bandits. For a while the house was silent, while the Americans cautiously closed in. Then Cardenas came out with his hands up, in token of surrender. As Patton moved forward to disarm him, the bandit chief treacherously pulled a gun and sent a bullet whistling past Georgie's tender left ear. That was his most foolish, and final, act. A split second later he lay dead in the dusty road.

Triumphantly, like a hunter back from a successful chase, Georgie returned to his general's headquarters with the bodies of three dead bandits tied to the running boards of the cars. Afterward he always referred to the battle at Rubio Ranch as the "first mechanized action of the United States Army."

CHAPTER 8

"MY TANKS...
GOD BLESS THEM!"

IN 1916 PRESIDENT WOODROW WILSON WAS REELECTED ON THE slogan "He kept us out of war." Bea voted in that election for the first time—for the Republican candidate, Charles Evans Hughes, who favored intervention on behalf of the hard-pressed Allies. She split her ticket, since Georgie's father, who had been District Attorney of Los Angeles, was running for United States Senator from California on the Democratic ticket. Isolationist Senator Hiram Johnson beat Mr. Patton easily.

Georgie never voted in all his life, because to do so would contravene his code of honor. As General Patton once expressed it, "I am in the pay of the Government. If I vote against the Administration, I am voting against my commander-in-chief; if I vote for it, I am merely bought."

• • •

The toy war in Mexico petered out in the spring of 1917, with Villa hiding in the mountains and President Venustiano Carranza's Mexican Government agreeing to put down banditry on the Border. But as the last shots echoed in the chaparral-covered ravines of Chihuahua, the uncontrollable forest fire of war leaped the Atlantic. On January 31, 1917, the Imperial German Government announced its decision to begin unrestricted submarine warfare. The American people, less inured to barbarity then than now, were outraged. The man of peace in the White House held them in check for two months while German U-boats torpedoed American merchantmen without warning, killing peaceful American citizens.

At last the President concluded that he could do no more. On April 2, 1917, he solemnly asked a wildly cheering Congress to declare war on Germany, saying, "The right is more precious than peace." It was a sentiment with which George Patton heartily concurred.

When General Pershing was named to command the American Expeditionary Force, he did not forget the keen young officer who had served him so well in Mexico. A secret telephone call in the night informed Patton that he was chosen to command Pershing's Headquarters Troop, the first contingent of the American army to sail for France.

Bea and Georgie started for Washington early the next morning. They remained there for a few hectic weeks and then went on to New York, from whence Pershing was to sail in great secrecy. To Bea it seemed that the secret was less than perfectly kept, since all the baggage was boldly marked:

> GENERAL PERSHING
> HEADQUARTERS TROOP
> *S. S. Baltic*

The moment for departure finally came. Bea, leaning from her hotel window, watched her husband walk off, swiftly, down a New York street with the sunshine flashing on his new captain's bars.

Pershing and the Headquarters Troop sailed for Europe on the old *Baltic* on May 28, 1917. The British greeted them with military fanfare and lodged them, as a signal honor, in the Tower of London. The French went wild when they reached Paris, and nearly buried them under gay spring flowers.

Once the bands stopped playing and the floral tributes ceased, Georgie got down to the hard work of organizing General Pershing's headquarters at Chaumont. He helped to set up a model military establishment capable of the tremendous expansion eventually necessary to direct an army of 4,000,000 men. By September the spadework was done, and Georgie became restless. He had no notion of sitting out the war on a staff job, and he began to put pressure on his favorite general.

Bea was at her family home in Pride's Crossing when Georgie's letter came, addressed to her father. Despite the ninety-five years he carried so spryly, Mr. Ayer was one of Patton's closest friends and most respected counselors. It was typical of Georgie to ask his advice on a question of great personal importance which, at the time, seemed of slight consequence in the vast pattern of history.

"I am offered the tanks or a brigade of infantry," Patton wrote: "Which shall I take?"

Mr. Ayer dictated the reply to Bea, who acted as his amanuensis: "I am a man of peace and know nothing of war, but I would advise you to take the command in which you can inflict the most punishment on the enemy while receiving the least casualties."

So Georgie chose the tanks. And, if he had the second sight he claimed, a certain unknown corporal in the Austrian army must have felt a cold wind touch his soul.

There were no American tanks. Nor were there any tankers.

On November 17, 1917, Captain George S. Patton, Jr., became the American Tank Corps. He spent eleven days at the French Tank School at Langres, and was then posted as American observer with the British at Cambrai.

As daylight seeped through the swirling fog on the morning of December 1, 1917, a new military era dawned. From the observer's post in one of the new British tanks, Patton could see a vast array of monstrous shapes waiting, silent and sinister, in a forsaken landscape. There were, he knew, 378 of the mechanical pachyderms waiting the signal to advance—it was the first large-scale tank attack in history.

The violent concatenation of the barrage fire slackened. A rocket spluttered through the fog, and taut young Englishmen glanced at their wristwatches. Then, with a vast outburst of sound, the land leviathans began slowly to move. They came to the front line of British trenches, teetered, and lurched forward, spanning the narrow ditches with their caterpillar treads. Clanking and groaning fearfully, they lumbered on. Their speed was a scant three miles an hour, but they moved. Irresistibly they moved! The loops and coils of barbed wire in desolate No Man's Land were squashed beneath their treads, enemy bullets flattened on their armor. Inside, the tanks were an inferno of smoke and gases; a hell of sound as their engines roared and the enemy fire beat a boilermaker's tattoo on their steel skins. But still they moved.

Now they came to the enemy trenches; and here they paused, astraddle the long, deep ditches, while their machine guns added to the din, mowing down the unprotected, crowded soldiers. Then they shuddered, as though at their own carnage, and moved on again.

Patton, peering through the observation slits, saw the Huns, their faces distorted in primeval terror; saw them fling their arms up in the futile gesture of surrender; saw panic sweep those battle-seasoned troops so that they dropped their guns and fled, screaming, in stampeding herds. And, as he watched, he knew that he was seeing the most epochal moment in land warfare since the first cannon breached a castle wall.

The British attack at Cambrai was too successful. The Germans were overwhelmed; but the attackers were so dumbfounded by the immensity of their success that they were paralyzed, unable to exploit it. As Patton said later, "The road to Berlin was as clear as a blasted parkway. But nobody knew how to use it."

The lesson was burned into Patton's brain by the fire and fury of that day. Thenceforward the tanks were his darlings.

• • •

Two weeks after the Battle of Cambrai, Patton organized the Light Tank School at Langres and was appointed its director. Almost simultaneously he organized and commanded the 302d Tank Training Center at Bourg. Patton was promoted to Major (temporary) in January, 1918. He took a busman's holiday of two weeks in May, to take part in the great French tank attack on the Montdidier-Noyon front. While commanding the Tank School and the Training Center, he was graduated from the Army Staff College at Langres.

Despite its great industrial prowess the United States failed to put a single American tank in Europe during that conflict. Patton's brigade was mounted in small, two-man French Renault tanks which, though more mobile, were far more vulnerable than the cumbersome thirty-ton British machines. When the French tanks arrived at the school, Patton was the only man who knew how to drive one. From noon until 2:35 A.M. he drove them off the flatcars and up to camp.

Then he wrote his daily letter to Bea, in which he commented: "The tanks will do 5 m.p.h. under good conditions."

Late in August, 1918, Patton organized the 304th Tank Brigade. His men were all volunteers and, in all their actions, they never lost a foot of ground, nor was a single man taken prisoner.

By now this transfusion of fresh American troops into the war-worn armies of France and Britain had turned the tide of battle. The last great German offensive was stopped dead at Château-Thierry on July 15, 1918, and three days later the Allies began the forward sweep which was halted only by Germany's surrender.

Until late August, American troops had been components of the Allied armies, commanded by foreign generals; but, on General Pershing's insistence, these troops were now gathered into the First American Army under his personal command. The object of the first all-American attack was a great bulge in the line, left by the retreating Germans, known as the Saint-Mihiel salient.

The offensive was set for September 12, 1918, and on August 22 Patton made a personal reconnaissance of the ground. Early in September he moved his tanks by train to their assigned position on the flank of the salient, around which three American Army Corps were posed to strike. It was reported to him that the French had missed the bridge by which his tanks were to cross the Rupt de Mad. Georgie was taking no chances—with his tanks. On the night before the attack he made sure the bridge was safe by crossing himself. Thus he earned his first D.S.C.

Before dawn on September 12 Georgie wrote to Bea, as he did every day come hell or high water. The closing lines of his letter read: "I am going into action now. My tanks are just coming over the hill, God bless them! I want you to know I have on all clean underwear."

So, clad in fresh raiment, fit to meet his Maker if he should be called, Georgie Patton led his little tanks into the first great American battle of the war.

Sputtering and back-firing, bucking like ill-trained cavalry mounts, 143 Renault tanks charged through the mist toward the German lines. Patton had decided that this new weapon should be used, like the armored cavalry of medieval times, to ride down the enemy's defenses and then sweep his rear. And that is what it did.

Unlike most field commanders of that era, who operated from nice, safe command posts, Patton rode in a tank in the first line of attack; for he ever believed that troops should be led, not driven. Some of his tanks were smashed by direct hits from the enemy 77's, some bogged down in oozy forest mud or stuck in ditches but enough kept going. Through Saint-Baussant to Essey they fought their way in a storm of rifle and machine-gun fire. . . and on to Pannes, which was the brigade's theoretical stopping place.

But Patton stayed there only for the night. The next day he pushed on without orders, testing his belief that tanks could operate, like Stuart's cavalry, in the vacuum behind the enemy lines. In its small way that daring sortie was the precursor and pattern for the swift tank sweeps of a later, greater war. It was the tactic used by Rommel when he cut France in two as he raced from Sedan to the Channel, and by Patton's own Third Army in the lightning dash that tore the Nazis' conquest from their weakening grasp.

For two more days Patton's tanks rampaged through the German backfield, knocking out machine-gun nests, taking prisoners, capturing astonished batteries of 77's who thought themselves safe behind the lines, and playing old hob with orderly German procedure. At one time he planted a little silk Stars and Stripes several miles behind the Hindenburg Line. On the third day the battle ended with the collapse of the salient under the pressure of half a million American troops, and Patton's tankers were sent rearward for a rest.

They rested about a week. Then, on September 26, they spearheaded the great final thrust of the war—the attack on the almost impregnable enemy positions in the forests of the hilly Meuse-Argonne country.

The high command had decided to hold the tanks in reserve

and let the 35th Infantry Division make the first attack along the Aire River. But, of all the plans of men, battle plans most often "gang agley." In the fury and terror of the predawn barrage and enemy counterfire, the green troops of the 35th became confused and lost; so Patton's tanks were ordered in to support the exposed flank of the 28th Infantry on the other side of the river. They came down the narrow strip between river bank and forest, with Patton, riding on top of a tank, shouting encouragement in his high-pitched voice that penetrated the uproar of battle.

But the Germans were getting wise to tanks. Patton's brigade was met by furious machine-gun fire, which did not stop them; but the accurate German artillery, posted for the purpose, hit them hard. Forty-three tanks were put out of action that day. A shell hit so close to Patton's tank that he afterward said, "I think I set a new record for the sitting broad jump."

After that, Patton walked beside the lead tank with a signalman to transmit his orders by the Boy Scout wigwag system.

Just before noon the remaining tanks stuck in a swamp close to Cheppy Woods. Patton, seeing that he was likely to lose his precious armor if the enemy should counterattack, ran back and rounded up a contingent of infantrymen. With blistering language, his six-guns swinging, he half drove, half led, them back to heave his tanks out by man power. As he came running forward, machine guns chattered from the forest and, in amazement, he felt the white heat of a bullet through his thigh— and fell down in an open field.

Joe Angelo, his runner, tried to pick him up, then dragged him to a shell hole. That fortunate depression in the ground became his command post. Between frequent fainting spells, as blood poured from his wound, Patton organized a line of defense, throwing out patrols to guard his precious tanks. Angelo carried his scribbled orders across the bullet-swept ground to his captains and lieutenants.

Patton never afterward remembered giving those orders; they were an almost automatic response to the necessities of the situation— "which shows," he often said, "the importance of constant training in every phase of warfare."

Then Major Sereno Brett, his second in command, came running to the shell hole. Patton relinquished command but insisted on being carried to the headquarters of the 35th Division to make his report. When that was done, he relaxed his tenuous grip on consciousness.

When he came to, Georgie was lying in the rain on one of a long line of stretchers. Nearby he could see the small tents of a front-line dressing station. People were moving about over there, but none of them came near him. As strength returned, he raised his head and looked at the other stretchers. Their occupants were clearly dead, and Georgie realized that he, too, was supposed to have gone West.

Thereupon the subdued decorum of that ambulance unit was shattered by such a burst of frightful language as never before or since has been uttered by any corpse.

Major Patton got attention fast.

Salem Bay was tranquil as a forest pool beneath the terrace of Avalon, where Bea sat reading the latest letter from her husband. It told of his promotion to full colonel (Temporary), jumping a grade, and of the Distinguished Service Cross that he had won. He was still in the base hospital at Alaret; but he expected to get out in a few days, for his convalescence had been rapid.

Too rapid, Bea thought. For a little while she had had no worry; now it would begin again. She put the letter down, and looked across the pastel shaded water to Misery Island floating on a diaphanous horizon. The stillness was so deep it seemed impossible even to imagine the din of war.

Then a church bell sounded strongly across the water— a wild, exultant ringing. Another joined it, and another—church bells, fire bells, school bells; all the bells of Beverly and Salem Town, Manchester and Revere, clanging across the water in a medley of joy.

Bea jumped up and ran into the house.

Irish William was standing by the telephone laughing and wiping his eyes. "Armistice!" he shouted. "It's the Armistice!"

The two little girls came running into the big marble hall. "What's armistice?" they chorused.

"Peace!" said Bea. "Praise God, it's peace! Now Daddy will come home."

CHAPTER 9

TANKS TO HORSES

MANY MEETINGS HAVE BEEN BETTER PUBLICIZED
than the one that took place at the Tank Center at Camp
Meade, Maryland, in March, 1919, but few have been more
fruitful. Colonel Patton, back from the wars, with his bright
new ribbons gleaming on his chest and his head bursting with
ideas about the proper utilization of tanks, encountered young
Lieutenant Colonel Dwight D. Eisenhower, who had commanded Camp Colt, at Gettysburg, which was the Tank
Training Center in the United States. Friendship flowered fast,
irrigated by mutual taste and enthusiasm for armored combat.

Young Eisenhower, round-faced and blue-eyed, looked like a
boy beside Patton, whose countenance was worn by the quick-
aging process of war. In some respects Eisenhower felt like a

boy beside the veteran officer, who had experienced so many things he knew only in theory. For Ike Eisenhower, to his great chagrin, had never yet heard a shot fired in anger.

Patton found that Eisenhower's brain was as good as his, and that the young man's knowledge of military history and of war technique equaled his own. Eisenhower, too, had a lot of very interesting ideas about tank warfare. For a while Patton occupied the position of mentor, then their discussions were between equals, as each stimulated the other.

Camp Meade had a lot of tanks for them to experiment with. Now that they were no longer needed, American tanks were pouring off the assembly line at Dayton and, in addition, British, French, and German specimens had been brought over for study. While the gasoline held out, the two men, with herds of tanks at their command, had a wonderful time testing their ideas in maneuvers over the Maryland fields. Then governmental economy shut off the food supply, and they were forced to confine their activities to theorizing. However they had a sound basis of fact and experience to go on; and their long, animated discussions shaped the future.

They were both extremely ambitious and, to increase their knowledge, each subscribed to the correspondence courses then being offered by the General Staff School at Fort

Leavenworth, Kansas. They made a practice of meeting at the house of one or the other and studying their lessons together. Thus their minds began to move in parallel grooves, and in later times each knew beforehand exactly how the other would react to a given situation.

Fast though the friendship grew, it was so deep-rooted that it never broke—not even under the sharp strains to which it was afterward subjected. In fact, it was an essential ingredient of the great victory in which they were to share the glory.

In the Army, war means action; peace means reaction. On June 30, 1920, two foreseen but extremely disagreeable events occurred. Patton was reduced to his permanent rank of captain—his colonelcy had lasted longer than most of the temporary promotions, for some of the officers had been handed their demotion papers as they passed the Statue of Liberty on their way home from the war. Worse, the Tank Corps was disbanded by Act of Congress; and the tanks were handed over to the infantry.

Patton was almost as earnest an advocate of a separate tank corps as was Colonel Billy Mitchell of a separate air force, and his arguments were of as little avail. He was given his choice of following the tanks into the infantry or remaining in the cavalry. When the tank people said, "We'll get you back when we need you," he chose the cavalry.

Patton was a captain for just one day. On June 1 he was made a permanent major, and ordered to command the 3d Squadron, 3d Cavalry, at Fort Myer.

Now began the long years of peace wherein lay the danger of vegetating, while the Army shrank and the chance to gain distinction in the Service seemed increasingly remote. Nevertheless they were pleasant years for Patton—obviously Georgie could not vegetate under any circumstances; his interest always had a razor's edge.

He went back to his old love for horses with all his youthful ardor. Polo, horse shows, hunting, and steeplechasing occupied most of his spare time. The two girls were growing up. Their father had great fun teaching them to ride. They always had perfectly schooled horses, for until after he died they never rode a horse he had not trained for them. He was a hard taskmaster, but strangely patient and understanding. He would go over and over a point until he was sure they had grasped it, and he took miles of movies to illustrate their faults.

Bea, Jr., says, "Of course, he screamed at us when we made a mistake; but we were used to that—it didn't bother us."

When they fell, only slightly hurt, his first question was, "Is your horse all right?"

That was to take their minds off their woes, and to teach them to look after their horses.

Sometimes the training was rather rigorous. At Scofield Barracks, in Hawaii, Ruth Ellen (aged eleven) was schooling a big, ill-mannered hunter while her father made movies. Again and again the horse refused a jump, while Patton shouted advice and a few harsh words.

Finally he roared, "Get off and I'll put him over."

Ruth Ellen obediently dismounted. As her father leaped into the saddle and angrily swung the horse at the fence, Ruth Ellen dropped to her knees and prayed, "Please, Lord Jesus, make him fall off."

Patton kept his seat, but the horse refused for the sixth time. Afterward nobody bore any ill will. The Pattons never cherished grudges.

Patton was very thoughtful in helping his children to regain their lost nerve after a bad accident. Once a horse ran away with Bea, Jr., on Massachusetts Avenue in Washington. It was a terrifying experience, with the big hunter wildly thundering over the slippery asphalt through the heavy traffic. Patton took out after his daughter with superb horsemanship and reckless disregard of danger. He finally stopped her horse in the best cowboy style and lifted her, shaking, from the saddle.

She lost all desire to ride for a while after that. Patton was very sympathetic, and did not push her until he saw she was almost ready. Then he coaxed her out again. One of the most important lessons the girls had to learn was how often you could get your nerve back.

Georgie was also very sympathetic about horse-show nerves.

When Bea, Jr., was to ride in her first jumping-class in a show, she said to him, "Daddy, I'm so nervous I'm afraid I'll disgrace the family."

"Don't let that worry you," her father said, and grinned. "Once when I was about to ride in a jumping class in Madison Square Garden I got so nervous that I ran out into the street and shot my lunch."

Patton had a psychological formula for winning in a horse show. He said, "If it's a military show, I wear civilian clothes; and if it's a civilian show, I wear dress uniform with all my medals."

Though he rode in the shows, as in everything else, all out to win, winning was not of the essence. He often said, "It doesn't matter whether you win or lose, as long as you do your damnedest."

Patton helped to whip up tremendous enthusiasm for Army

polo and at one time was one of the best players, with a six-goal handicap. In 1922 he was manager of the Army team which amazed everyone, including themselves, by winning the American Open Championship at Meadow Brook.

The team was quartered at the Army Polo Center at Mitchell Field, and Patton took that opportunity to learn to fly, in an old Curtiss Jenny.

The Army players were wined and dined in the great houses of the polo-playing Long Islanders. One night, as he was driving Bea home from a formal dinner, Georgie saw three men pushing a struggling girl into a furniture van on a dark road. He was out of his car in a flash, drove off the kidnappers at the point of a gun, and rescued the girl.

When a Meadow Brook friend asked how he happened to be armed, Patton said, "I believe in preparedness. I always carry a hand gun, even in white tie and tails."

Fox hunting was the only noncompetitive sport that Patton liked, but he became a fanatical devotee of that. On a later tour of duty in Washington he hunted strenuously with the Virginia packs. His wife finally got tired of sitting at home waiting for bad news and, at the age of forty, took up hunting. By then the girls were nearly grown, and splendid horsewomen. It was quite a sight to see Bea Patton with her two girl outriders tearing along on their big, half-bred hunters, with experienced youth giving neophyte age advice: "Slow up for the plow, Ma, and take the gate straight"—and the General roaring over his shoulder, "Come on, Bea! Do you want to live forever?"

By 1937 Mrs. Patton had become so accomplished a huntswoman that she was made Joint Master of the Cobbler Hunt, with her husband. It was the sort of triumph she loved best; for, as Ruth Ellen once said of her mother, "She's a Yankee, and doesn't think she is getting anywhere unless she has something to overcome."

Of her mastership of the Cobbler, Bea Patton wrote:

> *By then the moral victory over fear was far behind. Hunting, polo, dangerous sports, but they keep us intrepid; for in sport, as in all life, the big jump, if well taken, makes all the rest look picayune.*

CHAPTER 10

SALEM BAY TO
MAUNA KEA

AS IS THE ARMY WAY, THE PATTONS WERE SHIFTED
rapidly from place to place. Two years at Myer, then a tour at
Fort Riley in the Cavalry School. From there to Fort
Leavenworth, Kansas, where Patton was graduated with
honors from the General Service School. Then he was sent to
Boston, Massachusetts, as Assistant Chief of Staff, G-1, 1st
Corps Area, in July, 1924.

While Patton was still stationed in Kansas, Bea gave him a
son. George Smith Patton IV was born at Pride's Crossing on
Christmas Eve, 1923. Bea declared that it was the finest
Christmas present she had ever had, and her husband was
equally delighted.

However, Georgie was not obsessed by the idea of having a
son. His first concern was always for Bea. That she should
come through safely was all that really mattered.

Once, when she was carrying her third child, she asked, "Georgie, do you want a son very badly?"

Her husband smiled at her and said, "After all, I married a girl."

The nine months the Pattons lived in Boston, before being ordered to Hawaii, were a very happy period, and led to their decision to buy a home of their own in Massachusetts. During the first sixteen years of their married life they never owned a house, though they could well afford to do so. They lived in army cantonments or in tented houses while on duty, and preferred to spend their leaves visiting the Ayers or the Pattons; for both Bea and Georgie were devoted, not only to their own parents, but to their respective in-laws.

Indeed, Patton's affection for Mr. Ayer was second only to his love and respect for his own father. Georgie's intense devotion to Mr. Patton was another singular facet of his apparently contradictory character. When he was with his father he seemed almost to become a little boy again, so respectful was he to the older man. Even when he was a colonel, he always leaped to his feet when Mr. Patton entered a room. As long as they lived, the elder Pattons came to visit their son, wherever he was stationed, and he wrote to them every Sunday and Wednesday.

Though Bea and Georgie cheerfully accepted the nomadic life as inevitable in the Service, they decided, in 1926, to establish a home to which they could always come back from the far-off places of the world. That summer they purchased a farm in South Hamilton, Massachusetts, a few miles inland from Pride's Crossing.

Green Meadows is part of a lovely rolling countryside. The low, white, wooden house, standing close beside the road, seems small at first glance; but it rambles on, room following room at odd angles and up and down steps. There is a big formal drawing room, a dining room, a small parlor, and the General's den. From the hand-hewn beams of the raftered library hang all types of weapons and armor—a medieval knight's helmet; long Arab rifles, their stocks inset with mother-of-pearl; numerous swords and pistols, ancient and modern. Beside the fireplace are the spurs of General Cardenas.

The house looks over the green meadows—for which it is named—down a gentle slope to a pond. Beyond that is a gently rising hill where, in the early morning, hounds and huntsmen often show along the skyline.

On the Christmas after young George was born, George resolved to make his present the second best for Bea. When she came down to breakfast, she found a beautiful, black, thoroughbred mare standing with her head in the dining-room window.

Bea would not have been particularly surprised to find a horse in her house. In fact, horses were about the only pets that did not regularly live indoors, for the Pattons felt, unanimously, that "pets are no good unless they are members of the family."

On that basis the roster of the Patton family is long and curious. First came a bloodhound, named Barkis because he was so unwilling. Then Char Dassaut, who had come back from France with the tanks. At Fort Riley they had seventeen dogs including another bloodhound, named Flipper, who could eat a whole dinner off the table at one snatch. Judy, a German shepherd, founded a long line of descendants. There were three greyhounds—Golgo, Spareribs, and Sailor—and a bull terrier called Tootie, alias the Senator, who was reputed to be the editor of a sheet known as *The Doggerel*.

Two rabbits lived for a while on the porch roof. When one died Bea took the other into her room, where he kept her awake all night thumping for his mate. Fish, canaries, turtles, tame crows, kangroo rats, and coyote puppies were part of the ménage at different times. Once Mrs. Patton started on a trip with twenty-nine white mice and an aquarium.

The Pattons seemed fated to acquire animals. Once, when a dead baby chick was being buried amid loud lamentations, Ruth Ellen came out of the house, with her tears dried, and announced, "Mother, God has been very good to us. A perfectly strange cat has jumped in the window and laid six kittens on my Indian suit."

An especially eccentric member of the family was Lemoyne, a white duck with a yellow topknot, "who came to us in the desert at Fort Bliss." They sank a washtub in the lawn for him and, as special treats, turned on the sprinkler, which he loved.

One night Lemoyne disappeared in a rare thunderstorm. The Pattons, who were having guests for dinner, sent out a general alarm.

Just as the main course was served, the sergeant on duty at the gate of the fort telephoned: "Sir, Lemoyne has left the post and started downtown."

Leaving their food, Bea and Georgie and their company dashed out in the rain to the rescue; but not until the rain had stopped did they find Lemoyne, down by the railroad tracks, looking as foolish as could any old duck who had been out on a binge.

The brief interlude at home ended when Patton was ordered to Hawaii in March, 1925. Three years there as Assistant Chief of Staff, and then to the War College in Washington, and after that with the 3d Cavalry again. To Hawaii once more, followed by tours at Fort Riley and Fort Clark. Then to Fort Myer, as colonel commanding the 3d Cavalry, in December, 1938—his last peacetime post.

Wherever they went, the Pattons had fun. Mrs. Patton says, "Life on an army post is never dull." Life anywhere with Georgie was never dull. No matter how poor the assignment he drew, he always pretended that it was exactly what he wanted; and he threw himself into it full-force.

Patton made a multitude of outside interests for himself. As when Bea first met him, on Catalina, there was never enough time for all the things he wanted to do.

At Riley, Patton figured out the location of the Old Mormon Trail; then followed it with his family. On the first tour in Hawaii they explored the jungle hills, finding forgotten native temples. For springtime and summer in Washington, when there was no hunting, Patton invented a game which all the family could play. It consisted in fighting the battles of the Civil War over the original terrain.

The game was a very serious business, done with absolute accuracy. Each member of the family became one component of the contending armies—Mrs. Patton always had to be a

Yankee because she was one—and if a battle had lasted three days, the Pattons took three days to fight it. They reenacted Bull Run from Sudleigh's Ford to the gates of Washington, and Gettysburg from the first accidental clash of cavalry patrols to the last shot from Cushing's guns.

Ruth Ellen added a fine histrionic touch to the latter performance when, unconscious of a busload of startled tourists, she rushed out of the woods impersonating her great-uncle Tazewell Patton and, clapping her hand to her jaw, shouted, "My God, I'm shot!" Thereupon she fell writhing to the ground and, drawing pencil and paper from her pocket, scribbled, as had the gallant Confederate: "Here died General Tazewell Patton of Pickett's Brigade."

As young George grew up, he became very much his father's son—Patton saw to that, and he had a willing pupil. Once, when they were in Washington, George (aged five) came crying into the house, saying that a bigger boy had knocked him down.

"Get out of here, you yellow-bellied coward," his father roared, "and don't come back till you've beaten that boy up."

George followed his orders.

Like all the Pattons, George became a horse-show rider very early in life. In his first show he was mounted on a chubby little pony named Jeff. George rode proudly into the ring, then wheeled his mount and dashed back to his mother.

"I want to be sure I've got this right, Ma," he said. "If I win, I congratulate second, third, and fourth. If I get second, I congratulate the other three; and if I don't get anything, I congratulate everybody who gets a ribbon."

"That's the way your father always does," said Bea.

Sportsmanship was the guiding principle of Patton's training, and the family motto was: "You do your best, for if you don't you're better off dead."

All the children stayed in the Army. In 1934 Bea married young Lieutenant John C. Waters. In 1940, as the shadows of war closed in, Ruth Ellen married Lieutenant James Willoughby Totten. George, of course, went to West Point, where he followed his father's example even to the extent of failing in his plebe year and being set back a class.

For his second trip to Hawaii, Patton purchased the small gaff-rigged schooner *Arcturus* and shipped her to the West Coast. He studied navigation for two weeks with an old sailor in Washington, then announced that he was going to sail his yacht to Honolulu. Bea was game, and they took Georgie's boyhood friend Frank Graves and Mr. and Mrs. Gordon Prince along. A deckhand named Joe was the only professional aboard.

Of course both Pattons had considerable experience with small boats. On one occasion they had rescued three boys who had upset in a squall on Salem Bay. Bea had sailed their sloop while Georgie swam back and forth, three times, through the angry water towing a half-conscious boy to safety. Thus he gathered one more emblem of glory to wear on his chest, the Congressional Life Saving Medal.

Small boats in Salem Bay are one thing; an ocean crossing of 2200 miles is quite another, but Patton was confident. The first morning at sea, Bea tried to get breakfast but succumbed to seasickness. She was always sick on her husband's yachts; but she always went along, eventually overcoming her weakness by sheer will power.

Patton's first triumph as a navigator occurred after long days at sea when, busy with sextants, charts, and reams of scribbled figures, he announced, "We should sight land this morning."

Almost immediately Joe, in the crosstrees, sang out, "Land ho!"—and the peak of Mauna Kea lifted above the horizon.

The Pattons made another long cruise to Fanning Island and the Palmyras, and later sailed the *Arcturus* home from Hawaii. On both of these expeditions young George served as a paid deckhand. In order to qualify, he was obliged to get seaman's papers from the authorities in Honolulu.

Just before the war Patton acquired the ship of his dreams. She was the schooner *When and If*, especially designed around Georgie's own plans by the great New England yacht builder John Alden.

Even in his seafaring, Patton was not unmindful of his main purpose. He often said that someday he might fight with tanks in Africa, and would need to know celestial navigation in order to guide them across the trackless desert.

Whatever the Pattons did—hunting, fishing, or traveling; playing games or going to shows—they did together, as far as possible. No member of the family was ever left behind except by force of necessity. And whatever they did was done in the do-or-die spirit of Georgie's nature. They were all of one mind that way.

Should any of them be faced with a hard decision, he or she invariably resolved it in the light of Patton's favorite maxim, which he quoted on every apt occasion and by which he ordered his whole life. It was the famous phrase of Stonewall Jackson: "Do not take counsel of your fears."

CHAPTER 11

THE TANKS ROLL
AGAIN

IN SEPTEMBER, 1939, AT LEAST TWO MEN KNEW THAT the United States would fight again in Europe. One of them was President Franklin D. Roosevelt; the other was Colonel George S. Patton, Jr. Roosevelt had made up his mind in August of that year; Patton had known it for a decade.

And for twenty years Patton had been pleading for more tanks. How far it got him is shown by General Douglas MacArthur's final report as Chief of Staff in 1935, wherein he pointed proudly to the fact that the Army had just ordered twenty-seven tanks. Twenty-seven tanks for the whole United States Army, while Hitler marched into the Rhineland!

Patton was still commanding the 3d Cavalry at Fort Myer when the German armies swept through Poland in September,

1939. That was the blueprint for modern war, the rough pattern of the future. Patton, reading the War Department intelligence reports, visualized the mechanized columns slashing across the dusty Polish plains, and thought, "That is the way Ike and I planned it at Camp Meade."

The Government began to order a few tanks; but there was small alarm in the United States during the curious quiescence of the "phony war," while the French armies stood confidently in the Maginot Line and the Nazis did nothing—except gather themselves for a spring at the throat of France.

The blow fell on May 10, 1940. The Wehrmacht overwhelmed Holland and Belgium—that was, of course, expected. Then, with their screaming Stuka dive bombers, their magnificent 88 mm. field guns, and their new motorized infantry, the Nazis crashed through the French defenses at the twice-fatal city of Sedan, and loosed their tanks behind the Allied line.

Before taking off on that wild dash, General Erwin Rommel made a Patton-like speech to his tankers: "you will have no support. There will be nothing on your right flank, nothing on your left flank, nothing behind you. But Rommel will be ahead of you!"

Violating all the conventional maxims of war, Rommel's

Panzer divisions cut straight across France to the Channel and, curling northward, trapped the flower of the Allied armies, who had marched to support Belgium. Though the magnificent British evacuation at Dunkirk saved most of these men, the Battle of France really ended there—almost before it had begun.

The rhythmic crash of Nazi boots marching down the Champs Elysées shattered American complacency. A sort of panic swept the nation, and we began to arm in earnest.

"When we need you, we'll call you back to the tanks," they had said. Georgie Patton did not have long to wait. His own record of his military service reads: "To Fort Benning, Georgia, commanding 2d Brigade, 2d Armored Division, July 16, 1940. To—"

That is where his record ends. He never had an opportunity to complete it. So the dash after "To" stands for the long, crowded road from Benning to Indio, to Casablanca, to El Guettar, to Sicily, to England, to Brittany, to the Rhone, to Pilsen, to Victory—with the stars multiplying on his polished helmet, and the clanking, roaring tanks clearing the way.

Since his cadet days Patton had kept a list of men he would like to have with him when he got his army. You may be sure that every name in the little black notebook was that of a hell-for-leather fighter. Now he began to gather these men around him. From Fort Myer he took Major Hobart Gay and Captain Paul D. Harkins. Gay had lost an eye playing polo, and had gone into the remount service on being told he could never be promoted. Patton didn't care a hoot about a missing eye—Nelson did all right at Trafalgar. Harkins commanded a troop of 3d Cavalry with all the dash and swagger Patton loved. Gay and Harkins went with him all the way.

Richard Norman Jensen came to him at Benning, a young lieutenant just out of Officer Candidate School, with a loyal heart, a boyish, smiling face, the kind of humor Patton loved, and a bicycle named Junior. Patton made him an aide—and Jensen went as far as Tunisia, where a Nazi bullet stopped him.

One day at Benning, Alexander C. Stiller drove into the yard in a cheap, dusty little car. He was a tough, picturesque character who had been a sergeant with Patton in 1918.

When Bea came to the door, Stiller said, "Well, there's a war coming on."

Bea answered, "That's true. But who are you?"

"I'm Stiller. You know me. I've come."

Stiller had sold his small business in California and driven east to join his old commander. Patton sent him to O.C.S. and then made him an aide. Stiller, too, went all the way.

Another devoted friend who joined Patton at Benning was Colonel Geoffrey Keyes. Later Keyes was given a division, but he returned to Patton for Torch, the African invasion, and was Deputy Commander of Seventh Army in Sicily.

The first star twinkled on Patton's shoulder straps soon after he reached Benning. Another quickly followed it, and Major General Patton was posted to command the 2d Armored Division. It was, ever after, the outfit he loved best.

How he worked those civilians in uniform! They sweated out forced marches through the blazing Georgia summer, and froze in winter in what shelter they could find. In a few rickety tanks, in trucks marked "Tank," with logs marked "Gun," they maneuvered all over the Southern states. Patton was everywhere. When he found he could not get around fast enough in a jeep, he brushed up on his piloting and bought a little Stinson plane. Nobody in Second Army ever knew when the Commanding General would skim over the treetops and drop in, screaming, "Hurry up!" Patton's successful reconnaissances in his small sport plane led to the adoption of the Piper Cub for such contact work with troops.

Between the marches and maneuvers—even during them—the troops polished equipment and boots and helmets; pressed uniforms; washed linen; shaved every day—and cursed the General who made them do it.

Patton was disgusted with the coveralls supplied the tankers. They were loose and caught on knobs and nuts within the tanks, and were otherwise inadequate. So Georgie designed a tanker's uniform. It was green, for the color of oil, and fit as tightly as the skin of an eel. Georgie, riding half emerged from the turret of a tank, was a resplendent figure in his bright panoply, with a gold football helmet on his head and the ivory-handled six-guns strapped to his waist. The troops nicknamed him "The Green Hornet."

Patton built a tremendous amphitheater at Benning that would hold the whole division. There he regularly exhorted his men. Most of his speeches were sound military education; but they were liberally laced with four-letter invective, and enough references to gore and entrails to make the young recruits turn queasy: "When you put your hand in a blob of goo that a moment before was your best friend's face . . ."

The reporters loved him—and gave him the name by which he was always afterward known, though he hated it: "Old Blood and Guts."

His flash and toughness, and the fierce face that Patton wore, were part of an act. Once Nita asked her brother, "Why do you look so mean and ornery in your pictures?"

Georgie laughed. "That's my war face," he said.

Patton believed that a commander should apotheosize the fighting qualities of his troops. "Soldiers fight for two reasons," he said. "Hero worship for a commanding officer and the desire for glory. Patriotism is not enough. You can defend a position with patriots, but you can't take a position with them. The desire to do something heroic that will be long remembered will drive soldiers forward even to their deaths."

Perhaps Patton's greatest quality as a leader was his ability to infuse his troops with his own martial ardor. He could stamp his personality on a whole army and, though they sometimes hated him, they acted and thought and fought as he did.

By the fall of 1941 the 2d Armored was a real fighting outfit. In their shiny new tanks, with broad red, white, and blue stripes painted around the turrets, they roared through the great Louisiana maneuvers with a ferocity that was more than play-acting.

Then came Pearl Harbor, and the end of pretending. The chips were down, and the game begun. The 2d Armored was ready.

To Indio . . .

Up at the Operations Division of the General Staff, they were planning a possible invasion of North Africa. It might never be made; but if it were, it would be essential to have a large body of troops trained in desert warfare. Ike Eisenhower, head of Operations, felt that his old friend Georgie Patton was the man to do the job, and Secretary of War Stimson strongly seconded him.

So in March, 1942, Patton was called to Washington, shown the plan, and told to pick a place to train his army. He chose a huge tract of scorched and lifeless desert running from the Colorado River westward to Indio, California. There he could simulate the real conditions the troops would face in the great deserts of Africa. There he would toughen them until they were fit antagonists for Rommel and his hard-bitten Afrika Korps.

The rumor ran through 2d Armored that Patton was going to a new command. They had hated him, and grumbled and cursed him in Pattonian fashion. But somehow things looked different when they heard he was to leave.

Patton planned no farewell to his troops. He wanted to slip quietly away, and arranged to start, secretly, at noontime when the men would be at mess. The secret was not kept.

When he drove from his quarters in his command car, Patton saw an amazing spectacle. Soldiers were pouring out of their mess halls, leaving their sacred grub to line the road in triple ranks for miles. As he drove down the narrow lane between the wildly cheering men, a spontaneous inspiration, born of high emotion, swept their ranks. In a gesture symbolic of devotion his tankers tore their shirts off their backs and waved them at the stern, bespangled figure of their general. The car passed by so quickly that they could not see that the fraudulent old softy was crying.

CHAPTER 12

OUT OF THE DUST

THE ROUGH WOODEN STAGE STOOD IN THE MOJAVE Desert. Its backdrop was the High Sierras, sharp-cut against a cloudless sky. In front of it, thousands of men sat on the desert floor. They wore the uniform of the United States Army; but they were civilians still, despite their months of basic training. You could tell it by the way they sat, with shoulders slouched and bellies out; by sloppy uniforms and, most of all, by the slackness in their faces.

An olive-drab Army car came boiling out of a cloud of dust, and slammed to a stop behind the platform. Out jumped a gaunt, ramrod figure who ran up the short flight of steps. In the harsh sunlight he glittered almost painfully.

For a moment, while he stood against the vast background of

the mountains, he looked small and lonely. Then, by a conscious effort, he began to grow visible before their eyes until the mountains were forgotten and all they saw was the fierce old warrior glaring at them.

Suddenly, in a penetrating voice that rattled the loudspeakers and seemed to vibrate their bones, he addressed them: "Soldiers!"

The effect of that one word was startling. The crowd rustled and heaved as men sat a little straighter and furtively adjusted a cap or buttoned up a shirt. "Soldiers!" They hadn't thought of themselves as that before–not really.

The harsh, high voice went on, getting harsher, higher, and more penetrating. Dishing out stark reality in violent words. Telling them what to expect, in very certain terms. But never condescending–speaking as their commander, yet as one warrior to another.

"Soldiers!" he called them. And when the speech was finished, they *felt* like soldiers.

Before they left that desert, they were veterans. The training through which Patton had put 2d Armored was like a cub-scout hike compared with the conditioning he gave his new command. The country he had chosen for the maneuvers was like a lunar landscape whose fierce heat knows neither tempering shade nor any balm of growing things, where heat vanishes with the sun and—by comparison with noontime—nights are arctic. When the world is dead at last, it will resemble that Nevada desert.

All day and every day the troops marched, maneuvered, served the overheated guns, took tanks on endurance runs, dug slit trenches, laid mines, fortified mountain peaks, and comported themselves, in general, as though the Afrika Korps were just over there beyond Boulder Dam.

The temperature ran up to 120 degrees in the shade—if there was any shade. Inside the tanks it got to 140 or 150 degrees. The men were allowed one canteen of water a day—when that was gone, there was no more. They grumbled fiercely, but later this privation paid big dividends.

The dust swirled around the moving columns, penetrating but impenetrable. You couldn't see the vehicle next in line; you could only push blindly on through the gritty fog. It choked the men and the motors, and everything turned gray. They found means of keeping the engines running, and learned to breathe an atmosphere that was nine parts solid matter.

At the weary end of the day Patton made all his officers run a mile. He ran a mile and a quarter. Then he would throw himself down on the ground and sleep, while spiders, lizards, and bugs crawled over him unheeded.

At the end of July, orders came for Patton to fly to London to confer with Eisenhower. Bea and his orderly, George Meeks, helped him as he carefully packed the fine new uniforms that would be resplendent enough for the British capital. While the big transport planes stood waiting in the desert, he said farewell to his staff. Then he kissed Bea good-by, and took off.

In London, Eisenhower told his old friend that the invasion of North Africa had been definitely decided upon—Torch was its code name. American and British troops were to sail from the British Isles, through the perilous Strait of Gibraltar, to attack Algiers and Oran in the Mediterranean. Georgie was to command the Western Task Force, which was to sail directly from America and simultaneously attack Casablanca on the stormy Atlantic coast of Morocco.

Later, Patton was to learn that many of Eisenhower's advisers had objected to his appointment on the ground that he was too violent and unpredictable. Eisenhower paid them no heed. To him there was nothing unpredictable about Georgie. He felt he knew exactly how his friend would react to any situation.

Further, he knew that Patton's study of war embraced the entire subject: logistics, food, health, clothing, and weapons of all types from the bronze sword of the Achaians to the latest rocket gun. He knew, for instance, why sixteenth-century soldiers wore baggy trousers, and why puttees came in and why they were replaced by boots. He knew all about medieval armor and about the types of footgear worn by soldiers through the ages. His remark concerning this knowledge was: "I have to know; that's my business."

When people accused Patton of making snap decisions, he said, "I've been studying the subject of war for forty-odd years. When a surgeon decides in the course of an operation to change its objective, to splice that artery or cut deeper and remove another organ which he finds infected, he is not making a snap decision but one based on knowledge, experience, and training. So am I."

Eisenhower knew all this about Patton. He also knew that Georgie was loyal and fearless, and had utter integrity. He believed that Patton would handle the landings and anything thereafter with the considered daring that such a risky enterprise required.

Eisenhower said, "I must have Patton!"

On the day before the Western Task Force sailed for Africa, Georgie went to Walter Reed Hospital, in Washington, to see his old commander. General Pershing was sitting in an easy chair. Though his body was frail, his face had not entirely lost the stern, tight-lipped look that had made men call him Black Jack.

The old man was inordinately pleased by Patton's call in the midst of his great business. They talked about the invasion for a while, and later about the old campaigns.

When it was time to go, Patton stood up and said, "I came here to get your blessing, General."

Pershing's face softened wonderfully. "Kneel down, Georgie," he said.

Patton knelt beside the chair, and Pershing laid his transparent, wrinkled hand on Georgie's bent head. When the blessing had been pronounced, Patton stood up and snapped his hand to his bestarred cap in salute to his general.

The old man rose from his chair. Twenty years dropped from his shoulders as, standing erect, he returned the salute.

CHAPTER 13

"THE NICEST LITTLE FIGHT YOU EVER SAW"

ON THE MORNING OF OCTOBER 24, 1942, GENERAL Patton stood with Rear Admiral H. K. Hewitt and Captain Gordon Hutchins on the bridge of the heavy cruiser *Augusta* as she sailed between the mine fields of Hampton Roads. Beyond the Virginia capes a fleet of more than 100 warships, transports, supply ships, with the aircraft carrier *Ranger*, waited in five long columns. The *Augusta* took her place in the van, and the big convoy headed east.

Including the sailors 60,000 men were aboard that armada, of which 32,000 were troops of the Western Task Force under Patton's command. The long columns of dark gray ships looked impressive, but it was no great army with which to conquer half a continent. It was, in fact, hardly enough for a first-class parade.

Patton worried a great deal during the crossing—there were many things to concern a commander. It seemed hardly possible that the supposedly omniscient Nazi spy rings had not flashed the word back to Germany, and the question in most minds was: "When will the U-boat wolf packs strike?" Then the meteorological reports showed that, on an average, there were only twelve days in the whole year when the heavy Atlantic swells would permit a reasonably safe landing on the rocky Moroccan coast. Finally came the question as to how much resistance the superior French forces would offer, and whether Spain's pro-Nazi dictator, Francisco Franco, would permit Hitler's armies to march through his country to assault Gibraltar and sweep across the narrow strait to attack the American flank.

However, these matters had all been considered and provided for in the plans—as far as anyone can provide for the chances of battle. Until the event nothing more could be done, and Patton's mind was too well disciplined to fret about decisions already made. What really bothered him was that the food aboard the *Augusta* was so good that he began to gain weight. To counter this dire situation the General chinned himself ten times every morning, and then ran in place 480 steps (one quarter of a mile) in his cabin.

As the final phase of his meticulous self-preparation, Patton read the Koran through. "A good book, and interesting," was his comment.

Two A.M., November 8, was H-hour, D-Day, for the combined assault on North Africa. By the evening of November 7 the convoys from England had passed through the Strait of Gibraltar and assembled off Algiers and Oran. Eisenhower had established his headquarters in the fastness of the Rock. Patton's force, for the hazardous attack on the Atlantic coast of Morocco, was divided into three attack groups. Part of his beloved 2d Armored was to land at Safi, 150 miles south of Casablanca. The northern group, a task force of the 9th Infantry Division, was off Port Lyautey. The center, consisting of the 3d Infantry Division, CCB, 2d Armored, and most of the warships, headed straight for Casablanca, the only great modern Moroccan port, where lay a strong French fleet consisting of cruisers, destroyers, and the huge battle cruiser *Jean Bart*. As always, the *Augusta* was leading the way.

At ten-thirty that evening General Patton went to bed with his clothes on, and forced himself to sleep for three hours. "It was a hard thing to do," he declared.

Just before 2:00 A.M. Patton went up to the *Augusta's* bridge.

As he stepped out on deck, the characteristic sour-sweet smell of Africa made his nostrils quiver, while his eyes glinted with glee at the sight of unsuspecting Casablanca sleeping with her lights on. The sea, which had been stormy only two days before, was as gentle as an old polo pony, while lighthouse flashes from the looming headlands gave the invaders their exact bearings.

"I guess I must be God's most favorite person," Patton said exultantly.

All around him on the dark purple sea the transports lay motionless while men climbed down the nettings to the boats, and winches clanked and grumbled as they swung light tanks and the new 105 mm. mobile guns—which, with bazookas, were being used for the first time—into the landing craft. As each boat was filled, it sped off to join the immense circling group that awaited the moment of attack.

Patton, straining his eyes to watch them through the darkness, saw that roaring ring of assault craft deploy into line, abreast, and head for the dim beaches. For some time he could follow their course by the straight white wakes they left. Then they were lost in the shadows under the hills. For an eternity nothing happened. The lighthouses continued to flash steadily from the capes, and the lights of Casablanca, far to the right, twinkled peacefully. The landing beaches were shrouded in silence.

The battle began with a sputter of machine-gun fire and rifles popping like a string of Chinese firecrackers. Searchlights flared on Cape Fedhala, splashing their fierce white light across the beaches. Then the heavy coast-defense guns boomed, and a battery of old French 75's barked fiercely. The *Augusta* leaped forward as Captain Hutchins ordered her to close the shore, and the six eight-inch guns of her forward turrets blasted in unison.

Patton, watching the intermittent flashes of fighting on shore, said to Captain Hutchins, "I wish I were a second lieutenant again."

General Patton ordered himself to go ashore at 8:00 A.M.— it took all his self-control to wait that long. By seven-thirty his boat was swung out on the davits and loaded with his gear, including the white pistols.

A few minutes later Patton said to Dick Jenson, "Go get my pistols; I'll wear them now."

As Jenson went to the boat, a French cruiser and two big destroyers came tearing up the coast, close inshore, trying for the transports. The *Augusta* surged forward at twenty knots, and her rear turret swung until the guns pointed over Patton's landing boat. The triple blast from their muzzles blew it to pieces, but Jenson already had the precious pistols.

For the next three hours there was a wild naval melee, with all the American ships zigzagging at full speed and firing as fast as they could at the French warships that dodged in and out of Casablanca. Enemy bombers joined the fray, and the *Jean Bart*, which had been sunk at her dock in shallow water by a broadside from the battleship *Massachusetts*, continued to lob enormous fifteen-inch shells into the battle. One of them exploded in the water so close to the *Augusta* that Patton, standing on the main deck, was drenched by the splash.

Though the naval fighting was fun to watch, Patton was wild to get ashore. This sort of thing was the admirals' business.

By twelve-thirty the French ships were either sunk or disabled, and at 1:20 P.M. General Patton hit the beach. Harkins was there to greet him as he emerged, dripping, from the surf.

The Deputy Chief of Staff reported considerable confusion. Some of the men were hanging back and taking cover instead of unloading the landing craft. The beach was under artillery fire, and French planes, still in command of the air, strafed it continually. Thereupon Patton, very erect and soldierly, walked slowly down the beach. He was quivering inside, for the thing he feared and hated most was being strafed from the air. But he had to do it, because he believed that in moments of crisis a commander should be seen by his men. With the white pistols hanging at his hips, the sun blazing on his ribbons and on the bright stars on his helmet, Patton might have been the modern embodiment of Caesar in his scarlet battle cloak or the white plumed helmet of Navarre.

And his tactic worked. The troops stopped diving into foxholes every time they heard the roar of a motor, and steadily unloaded the landing craft—you felt pretty foolish cowering on your stomach while your commander-in-chief walked nonchalantly along the beach, not seeming to notice that anybody was shooting at him.

That night Patton and Harkins and Gay slept for a few hours in a little beach house. The countersign for the day was "George" and the reply was "Patton."

The General was awakened by a sentry barking in a hoarse voice, "Halt! Who goes there? George!"

A soft Chinese voice replied, 'Me no George! Me Thue Lee, best damn cook in U. S. Army."

Patton burst out of his house shouting, "Grab that man! If he's the best cook in the Army, I want him."

Evidently Sergeant Thue P. Lee was not boasting, for he was Patton's personal cook throughout all his campaigns.

In the morning varying reports came in. Brigadier General Lucian K. Truscott was having a stiff fight at Lyautey. General Ernest N. Harman had the 2d Armored safely ashore and was coming up the coast against serious resistance. But the 3d Division was stopped dead, and the battery of 75s on Cape Blondin was still shelling the beach. Patton jumped into a light tank and personally organized the attack that took the battery.

The French in Casablanca refused an armistice and continued to fight desperately. Patton hesitated to order a direct assault because of the many lives, American and French, it would cost.

On November 10—D-Day + 2—he got a message from Eisenhower:

> *Dear Georgie:*
> *Algiers has been ours for two days. Oran defenses are crumbling rapidly with naval shore batteries surrendering. Only tough nut to crack is in your hands. Crack it open quickly.*
> IKE

That was all Georgie needed. He ordered an all-out assault for 7:30 A.M. on November 11, 1942—his fifty-seventh birthday.

The warships were in position, with their guns trained, the troops straining at the jump-off points, and the bombers actually circling their targets, when French General Auguste Noguës sent an officer through the dim morning light to surrender Casablanca.

Patton gladly accepted it, and notified Eisenhower that his mission was accomplished. He treated General Noguës to a champagne breakfast, gave him a guard of honor, and ordered that the gallant French be accepted, thenceforward, as Allies.

To his commander-in-chief at Algiers, a few days later, Patton gave this lighthearted report of the battle: "Say, Ike, it was the nicest little fight you ever saw. And I've got the greatest army that ever was. Julius Caesar couldn't be a brigadier in it!"

CHAPTER 14

PATTON ANSWERS
AN SOS

FOR THE NEXT THREE MONTHS PATTON WAS OUT OF the fighting; but, though he hated inaction, he managed to enjoy himself at Casablanca, which he described as a combination of "Hollywood and the Bible." His job demanded that he establish friendly relations with the French and with the Sultan of Morocco, and he carried it out with his usual dash. General Noguës and his officers entertained no hard feelings toward the victor; in fact, they regarded him with respectful admiration. The French seemed to feel that they had somehow regained their lost honor by putting up such a stiff resistance, and one of them told the American general that they were "delighted to have fought with him in a friendly manner."

Patton considered this a rather curious phrase in view of the fact that the French had lost nearly 3,000 men, killed in action, and the Americans had some 700 casualties.

The meetings with the Sultan were a series of splendid, barbaric pageants staged in the ruler's magnificent palaces at Marrakech and Rabat. These elaborate oriental pleasure domes had interiors decorated in brilliant mosaics and exquisite filigree work. Troops of Moorish cavalry mounted on white stallions and wearing white capes, with blue hoods thrown back over red coats agleam with gold braid, and snowy white turbans, clattered beside the General's car as his guard of honor, while mounted bands played modern marches on ancient oriental instruments. The meetings usually ended in a terrific banquet of twelve courses or more. But Patton was too busy now to have to worry about his waistline.

The Sultan, a handsome young man who spoke perfect French and English, admired the American General extravagantly. Patton seemed to him the modern incarnation of the ancient virtues of his warrior ancestors. Even when the rulers of the world gathered at Casablanca, and Churchill, Roosevelt, Eisenhower, Montgomery, Alexander, Tedder, and Lord Louis Mountbatten paid their respects to the titular ruler of Morocco, that perverse young man continued to regard Patton as the greatest of them all.

After a boar hunt, in which the American shot an old tusker through the eye at such close range that the beast's dying rush spattered blood all over his uniform, the Sultan presented Patton with the order of the Grand Cross of Ouissam Alaouite (The Hunter), which carried the citation: "The lions in their lairs tremble at his approach."

Meanwhile, 1200 miles to the east, the Allied forces under Eisenhower were fighting desperately in Tunisia. Their first rush toward Bizerte and Tunis was stopped dead by Colonel General Juergen von Arnim's veteran German divisions, which poured across the narrow Sicilian straits. Then General Sir Bernard Montgomery's victorious Eighth Army came up the Libyan coast from El Alamein, herding the famous Afrika Korps, under the great Rommel, before it. Rommel's army turned at bay on the Mareth Line, and the "Desert Fox" detached two Panzer divisions to wipe out those annoying Americans on his flank.

They almost succeeded. The German armor, bursting suddenly out of the passes in the coastal range of mountains, overwhelmed the green American troops and drove them in confusion through Kasserine Pass. Eisenhower and General Sir Harold Alexander rallied their men, and they stopped the

German rush just short of the Allies' great forward base at Tebessa. It was a close call—too close for comfort.

Eisenhower, tired of fumbling and indecisive leadership, sent for Patton to take over the American 2d Corps and its shattered armor.

Patton was now in direct command of all the American troops actually fighting the Germans—there were only three divisions, the 1st and 9th and the 1st Armored, and a regiment of Rangers. They became the veteran cadre from which evolved the six great American armies that finally crushed the Nazis.

Patton's immediate superiors were the brilliant General Alexander and, of course, Eisenhower.

The first thing Patton did was to get the feel of his army. He did not like what he found. The two infantry divisions had too little battle experience, and the 1st Armored had had too much. The latter had been badly mauled by Rommel's Panzers. Half their equipment had been lost in the rout at Kasserine Pass, and they were weary of fighting the superior German tanks and artillery. They looked worn out, sloppy, and discouraged. On the other hand, they were battlewise veterans who knew the score. All they needed was confidence and pride to make them an elite outfit equal to the best Rommel had. Patton gave them back their manhood.

One of his favorite maxims was: "Sloppy soldiers don't win battles." The famous orders went out: helmets were to be worn at all times, neckties ditto, legging and side arms according to regulations. "Every man who is old enough will shave once a day." A howl of anguish went up from the troops, but they obeyed—or else!

Meanwhile Patton raced around his vast desert area making his famous fighting speeches. They went over like lead balloons. One wounded Ranger cracked wearily, "His guts and our blood." At this point Patton was probably the most unpopular commander in American history.

But something happened to 2d Corps. It became, in spite of itself, a Patton army—the first one—tough and bitter and proud; capable of doing the impossible, and then going out next day and doing it again.

The proof came shortly after the middle of March. Patton's army had fought its way back to the line they had held before the defeat in February, and Rommel decided to pull another Kasserine and finish them off for good. On a beautiful sunny day the Tiger tanks of his 10th Panzers charged out of the mountain passes and across the gay carpet of spring flowers on the desert floor. Each tank was assigned its individual mission of destruction as it headed for the American lines on the ridge behind El Guettar. The maneuver was almost the same as before, but it had a vastly different result. American guns, served by coolly competent artillerymen, blasted the Nazi column; American tanks countercharged valiantly. Within a matter of moments half the German tanks lay smoking on the plain, and the rest were fleeing to the safety of the hills.

Patton was wildly elated. For the first time, American armor had met the best the Germans had—and stopped it cold.

In the final stages of the Tunisian campaign 2d Corps proved its valor decisively by fighting its way across the mountains to Bizerte in the teeth of everything the Nazis could throw against it. General Patton did not command it in the victory drive—Eisenhower had transferred him to the more important task or organizing Seventh Army for the invasion of Sicily.

Patton went to his new command with a heavy heart, for he had suffered two great personal losses.

Young Bea's husband, cocky Colonel Johnny Waters, was listed among the missing. Patton himself searched the hills of Sidi-Bou-Zid for a grave, and found none; so he held to the hope that Waters had escaped. He was very proud of his son-in-law, for the men of Waters' command told how he had formed a rearguard, along with five other men, and held a hilltop against an overwhelming Nazi attack until the remainder of his outfit escaped.

Later, Waters turned up as a German prisoner of war; but for the duration of the war Patton took over the job of father to his two young Waters grandsons, writing them humorous letters every week and sending them such a collection of souvenirs that they were the envy of all their friends. Every night when the Waters boys said their prayers, they ended with, "And God bless old Blood and Guts."

An even greater blow was the loss of Dick Jensen, with his ardent loyalty and sunny humor. He was killed a few days after El Guettar, where Patton had promoted him, on the field, to Captain. When Patton heard the news, he stood immobile in his tent with tears streaming from his eyes. He loved Dick as much as his own son.

When, after many weeks of arduous training, Seventh Army stood poised for the Sicilian attack, General Patton took a day off. He flew from Algiers to Tunisia, and went to where his aide was buried. Getting out of his jeep alone, Patton walked through the desert gathering wild nasturtiums. Then he knelt beside the grave and tendered his gift of remembrance to Dick Jensen.

CHAPTER 15

THE FIRST BREACH

THE ADMIRAL'S BARGE PULLED AWAY FROM THE
command ship *Monrovia* and headed for Red Beach No. 2
with spray flying over her bow. General Patton stood in her
stern swaying easily to the rough motion of the boat, peering
intently at the shore ahead.

It was D + 1, the second day of the Sicilian invasion, and the
situation was critical. On the southeastern point of the island
Montgomery's Eighth Army was having an easy time, and at
Licata the Third American Division and Combat Command A
of the 2d Armored were safely ashore. But here at Gela, where
waves kicked up by the storm two days ago still smashed

powerfully against the rocky coast, there was trouble. The 1st Division and the Rangers were pinned down. It was not a beachhead at all, only a thin strip of ground between the hills and the sea—a toehold.

Patton noted the crumpled landing craft and the DUWKs stranded in the breakers, the flash and smoke of shellbursts on the beach, and the dust and streamers of fire rising from the little town of Gela. As the keel of his boat grated on the gravel, he jumped out, followed by Colonel Gay, and waded through the foam that soaked and blackened his shining cavalry boots. Behind him shells from German 88s lifted columns of white water from the blue sea.

A scout car was waiting for him; and he drove into Gela on his way to see Major General Terry Allen at 1st Division head-quarters, three miles to the east. As the car rattled through a narrow cobbled street, Patton saw the flag of Colonel John Darby, of the Rangers, flying from a small whitewashed house.

"Stop here!" he ordered.

They found Colonel Darby in the front parlor amid a clutter of plush furniture, field telephones, and maps strewn on the floor.

"Hello, Jack," Patton said. "I'm on my way to see Terry Allen, but I thought I'd drop in and see how you are doing."

Colonel Darby smiled thinly. "Lucky you did, General. Seven Nazi tanks have broken through between us and headquarters. You'd have run into them head on."

"I'm always lucky," Patton said. "What's the situation here?"

"We're under heavy attack by large numbers of German and Italian troops. I'm standing them off with two companies of Rangers, a battalion of engineers, a mortar company, and a battery of German 77's that we captured yesterday. If we don't run out of shells for the German guns, we may be able to hold out."

"Where the double-asterisks is Combat Command B?" Patton demanded.

"I don't know," said Darby, "but they sure would be useful here."

"Let's go out and look things over," Patton suggested.

"It's pretty hot out there, sir."

"I'm still lucky. Come on."

They went to a forward observation post about 100 yards behind the front line. From there Patton could see the enemy moving in a field a few hundred yards away. They were being held up by three American half-tracks—a vehicle never intended for front-line combat. Darby and Patton waited until they were sure the attack was stopped, temporarily at least, and then went back to Ranger headquarters.

The situation was dusty in Gela. A battery of 88's had just opened on the town. Ranger headquarters was hit twice, and the roof was blown off the house across the street. To add to the disorder, two misguided British fighter bombers dumped their loads into the main street. The noise of crashing shells was almost drowned by the high-pitched screaming of hundreds of frightened civilians. It was the nadir of the invasion—the brink of disaster.

Then a new noise augmented the clamorous confusion—the sound of heavy motors and the clank of armor. Patton dashed out of the house, and saw a column of newly landed American tanks coming up the street. Grabbing the officer in command, he ordered him to fight his way through to 1st Division and restore the line.

Soon the seven German tanks were destroyed, and Darby's Rangers counterattacked. The road to 1st Division was opened, and Patton mounted his scout car and started off to see General Allen.

Allen was coming in to see him, and the two generals met on a hillside. They discussed the situation, and Patton issued fresh instructions. While they were talking, fourteen German dive bombers came up the road; and the conference hastily adjourned to a ditch.

It had been a full day, the General thought as he started back for the beach; but he was confident. The crisis had been passed. His sense of well-being amused him, for even then his car was following a road that lay *between* the front lines of the two contending armies.

He reached the beach without incident, but his day was not yet done. While he was waiting for his boat, he saw that the soldiers on the beach had dug foxholes among piles of 500-pound airplane bombs.

He walked over to them and said, "You're just a great help to the Graves Registration."

"Yes, sir," said a corporal.

A flight of Messerschmidts came over the beach a few minutes later and, despite Patton's warning, the soldiers dived back into their suicidal foxholes. The General, controlling his jumping stomach nerves, made his usual nonchalant stroll along the beach, and shamed the men into coming out to the comparative safety of the open.

Sicily was taken in thirty-eight days. While Montgomery's Eighth Army slugged its way through the mountainous eastern end of the island, Patton made the first of those brilliant wheeling dashes for which he became famous. He threw a spearhead under Geoffrey Keyes across country to take Palermo and cut off the whole southwestern part of the island. Then he swept ahead, turning the flank of the forces confronting Montgomery. On August 17, 1943, British and Americans entered Messina as the last enemy troops fled across the narrow strait to Italy.

During the whole thirty-eight days Patton was in constant action. He averaged four hours' sleep a night and for twenty hours a day he stormed around Sicily, in jeeps, tanks, scout cars, and planes, visiting almost every unit of his army and every field hospital on the island. These hospital visits were the greatest strain he had to bear. He would walk through the aisles with tears pricking at his eyelids, hardly able to speak in his emotion.

On August 3, 1943, General Patton drove down from the mountains where 1st Division was fighting the last and bloodiest battle of the campaign. Though he looked, as ever, the hard-boiled, immaculate warrior, he was desperately tired and his soul was sick of blood. Despite his exhaustion he ordered his driver to take him to the 15th Evacuation Hospital at Sant' Agata.

Stepping wearily from his jeep, he entered the long ward tent and walked slowly between the line of cots. The stagnant air was heavy with the sick, sweet smell of putrid flesh, and the weird green light filtering through the canvas made the wounded boys look like living dead.

"How's the war going?" they asked, and he answered, "We're winning. You'll be out of here for the surrender."

In one bed a boy was dying. Patton answered his unspoken wish, holding his hand for a moment; then, lighting a cigarette, he put it between his lips and passed on, too moved to speak.

Nearly at the end of his tour Patton came upon a man sitting on the edge of his cot fully dressed with his helmet liner on.

"What's wrong with you?" he asked.

The boy looked up with tired, frightened eyes. "I guess I just can't take it," he said.

Those words, to Patton, were unforgivable—the final betrayal of his Spartan creed, which utterly condemned the weakling who "can't take it," and thus throws a double burden on the man who must fight for two. All the repressed worries that a general in command must never show—the strain of life-and-death decisions, the fear of death that must each day be conquered, the strain of going on in utter exhaustion, and the terrible emotional impact of those long rows of shattered men—burst loose in a terrible rage against this boy who had seemingly lost his manhood.

The General's high-pitched voice rose to a scream as he

cursed the unhappy soldier with all his famous fluency. And when even his command of language failed to express his loathing, he slashed his gloves across the soldier's face and knocked his helmet liner off.

Doctors and nurses hurried up and somewhat calmed the General, who stalked off muttering about "yellow-bellied cowards." The soldier dropped his head in his hands and cried.

Patton regretted his outburst at Sant' Agata mainly because it endangered the career he passionately loved. He never felt that he had been unjust. There had been much malingering in Sicily—and he could see his army melting away, for such behavior spreads through troops like a prairie fire. It was true that the slapped soldier, Private Charles K. Kuhl of the 26th Infantry, was really ill of malaria; but in Patton's book no man, however badly off, could say "I can't take it," especially in a hospital where men around him—men with shattered arms and legs, or bellies packed with dressings—could laugh and joke.

Patton himself was not a fearless man, but he held that "the strength of the soldier is fear of fear." Bea says that had she or any other member of the family behaved like Private Kuhl, he would have given them the same treatment— "and rightly so," she adds, with fire in her eye.

General Eisenhower took a different view. He felt that Patton's conduct was unjustified and morally wrong. For nights he lay sleepless wondering what he should do. Ike loved Georgie Patton, but he was determined that friendship should not influence justice. A more compelling reason forced his decision—"I can't afford to lose my best general," Eisenhower said.

The Commander-in-Chief wrote the sharpest letter of his life to General Patton, describing his action in scorching terms and ordering him to apologize, publicly, to Kuhl, to the nurses and doctors at the hospital, and to the whole Seventh Army or as much of it as could be reached.

Patton performed this duty with all the abandon of his nature and with all his flare for the dramatic. He humbled himself before Seventh Army in a series of public speeches to men of all ranks. The apology, freely given, was as freely accepted. Patton actually gained popularity by the incident. Eisenhower's report states that "[since then] it has been reported many times that in every recent public appearance of Patton before . . . his own soldiers he is greeted with thunderous cheers."

The slapping had one other beneficial effect that is not generally known. Patton became very conscious of the real danger of battle fatigue. He made a study of it and, as a result, when he commanded Third Army he saw to it that men showing signs of the strain of combat were given instant and effective treatment. There were rest centers everywhere in Third Army territory. Some were in great châteaux and castles taken over from the European aristocracy; others were no more than caves or deep dugouts within a few yards of the front. But, at the worst, they were places where a shaken man could stay, safe and warm, and rest until his courage was restored.

When the Sicilian campaign ended, Seventh Army was in effect disbanded. Its components were cannibalized to reinforce General Mark Clark's Fifth Army in the invasion of Italy, or sent to England to prepare for the great big D.

With his army being dismembered, Patton called his staff together. He appeared before them in his usual burnished splendor and, taking his place at the head of the table, said, "Gentlemen, I fear you have hitched your wagons to a falling star. However, I still have some influence left and I will see to it that anyone who wants to leave me will get a good job suitable to his rank and merits.

"I am not being relieved in this theater, but am being sent on another mission. If any of you feel so inclined, I'd like to have you with me."

He stood there, looking as stern as a Roman emperor in bronze, waiting for their reply.

Out of twenty-four men in the room, twenty-four said they would go with him. When he heard their reply, the General wept.

CHAPTER 16

LETTER ON D-DAY

ON THE MORNING OF JUNE 6, 1944, LIEUTENANT General George S. Patton, Jr., Commanding General, Third Army, sat in an ancient country house in the English Midlands writing to his son at West Point. That letter was a sort of spiritual last will and testament, though Patton's year of glory— the year for which he had been born, for which he had trained all his life—was just beginning.

Dear George:
At 07.00 this morning the B.B.C. announced . . . the landing of Allied paratroopers. . . . So that is it.
This group of unconquerable heroes, whom I command, are not yet in, but we will be soon—I wish I were there now as it is a lovely sunny day for a battle. . . .

I have no immediate idea of being killed, but one can never tell and none of us can live forever. So if I should go don't worry, but set yourself to do better than I have.

All men are timid on entering a fight, whether it is the first fight or the last fight. . . . Cowards are those who let their timidity get the better of their manhood. You will never do that because of your bloodlines on both sides. . . . Your knees may shake, but they will always carry you toward the enemy. Well, so much for that.

There are apparently two types of successful soldiers— those who get on by being unobtrusive and those who get on by being obtrusive. I am of the latter type and seem to be rare and unpopular, but it is my method. One has to choose a method and stick by it. People who are not themselves are nobody.

To be a successful soldier you must know history. Read it objectively—dates and even minute details of tactics are useless. What you must know is how man reacts. Weapons change, but man, who uses them, changes not at all. To win battles you do not beat weapons—you beat the soul of enemy man. . . .

You must read biography and autobiography. If you will do that you will find that war is simple. Decide what will hurt the enemy most within the limits of your capabilities and then do it. TAKE CALCULATED RISKS. That is quite different from being rash. My personal belief is that if you have a 50% chance you should take it, because the superior fighting qualities of American soldiers led by me will surely give you the extra 1% necessary. . . .

You cannot make war safely, but no dead general has ever been criticized, so you have that way out always. I am sure that if every leader who goes into battle will promise himself that he will come out either a conqueror or a corpse, he is sure to win. . . . Defeat is due not to losses but to the destruction of the souls of the leaders. The "live to fight another day" doctrine.

The most vital quality a soldier can possess is SELF-CONFIDENCE, utter, complete, and bumptious. You can have doubts about your good looks, about your intelligence, about your self-control, but to win in war you must have NO doubts about your ability as a soldier.

What success I have had results from the fact that I have always been certain that my military reactions were correct. Many people do not agree with me; they are wrong. The unerring jury of history, written long after both of us are dead, will prove me correct.

Note that I speak of "military reactions." No one is born with them any more than anyone is born with measles. You can be born with a soul capable of correct military reactions or a body capable of having big muscles, but both qualities must be developed by hard work. . . .

Soldiers, in fact all men, are natural hero worshipers; officers with a flare for command realize this and emphasize in their conduct, dress, and deportment the qualities they seek to produce in their men. . . . The troops I have commanded have always been well dressed, been smart saluters, been prompt and bold in action, because I have personally set the example in these qualities. The influence one man can have on

139

thousands is a never-ending source of wonder to me. You are always on parade. Officers who, through laziness or a foolish desire to be popular, fail to enforce discipline and the proper wearing of equipment, not in the presence of the enemy, will also fail in battle; and if they fail in battle they are potential murderers. There is no such thing as "a good field soldier." You are either a good soldier or a bad soldier.

Well, this has been quite a sermon; but don't get the idea that it is my swan song, because it is not. I have not finished my job yet.

Your affectionate father,
GEORGE S. PATTON, JR.

CHAPTER 17

LUCKY

IN THE ALLIED BATTLE CODE EACH OF THE ARMIES had a secret name. Most of them were high-sounding. SHAEF was called "Liberty," Twelfth Army Group was "Eagle," First Army was "Master." Patton prophetically named Third Army "Lucky."

Third Army was lucky, for the reason that it was molded in the image of its general—tough and cocky and daring, ready to take advantage of every break. And very proud of itself! When you asked a soldier of First or Ninth or Seventh Army what outfit he belonged to, he said "Third Division," or "Fifth Armored," or named some regimental unit. But one of Patton's men always answered, with a swagger, "Third Army."

Though Third Army was made up of infantry, artillery,

engineers, and all the other branches of the service, in addition to the armored divisions, it was in effect a cavalry army—the mechanized armored cavalry that Patton had envisaged. They never walked when they could ride, and they rode far and fast. Most of the staff were former cavalry officers whose names had been in Patton's little black book. They wore high, shining boots and the cavalry swagger; and their military thinking was a fluid as that of Genghis Khan, who conquered most of Asia and Europe with his wild Mongol horsemen.

From the moment he took over in England, Patton put his stamp on Third Army. The first directive in his Letter of Instructions No. 1, to his field officers, is the payoff:

COMMAND

A. Leadership
1. Full Duty

Each, in his appropriate sphere, will lead in person. Any commander who fails to obtain his objective, and who is not dead or severely wounded, has not done his full duty.

Third Army was Patton's baby, and he had paid a price, in pride, for it—the price of serving under Omar Bradley, who had been his junior in Sicily. In December, 1943, Eisenhower had sent for Patton to come to his headquarters in Tunis.

After dinner in the new Supreme Commander's little white villa on the Gulf of Carthage, Eisenhower said, "Georgie, I'm going to take Brad as my next senior officer. That means everyone else will be under him. If you want to go on that basis, I'll be glad to have you as an Army commander."

Patton instantly replied, "Yes. That's my job, Army Commander."

At 10:25 A.M., July 6, 1944, exactly a year to the minute from the day he left Sicily for Algiers, General Patton took off for Normandy. As his plane flew along the Cherbourg peninsula, the sea beneath it was a floor of ships carrying his army to France. He landed near Omaha Beach, where the wreckage appalled him. But he records that it "demonstrates good troops can land anywhere."

Patton's first command post in France was set up in an apple orchard at Nehou. There were three six-wheeled trucks with trailer bodies. One belonged to Major General Hugh J. Gaffey, his Chief of Staff; Gay had another. The third was for General Patton. Its interior was like the bare, ascetic cubicle of a plebe at West Point. It contained a small folding table; a cot, neatly made up army style; a small bookshelf. Among the books was the Holy Bible (usually left open), a volume of Kipling's poems, a life of Jeb Stuart, and Webster's Collegiate Dictionary. Like Napoleon, Patton never spelled too well—though sometimes he misspelled purposely; for example, he always spelled SHAEF as CHAFE.

There was also a bed for Willie, the white bull terrier Patton had acquired in England, who was his constant companion.

On his first Sunday in France, Patton went to the Catholic services. As he knelt with the troops in the muddy field, a massed flight of bombers drowned out the Latin prayers; and the air was shaken by the concussion of their bombs on the enemy lines a few miles away.

Patton hated the weeks he spent in the apple orchard while Montgomery's British and Canadians and Bradley's First Army slugged their way through the Bocage to the line of Saint Lo-Caen, near the neck of Normandy, from which Eisenhower planned to break out of the beachhead. Georgie was obsessed by the idea that the war might end before he ever got into it.

He need not have worried. The Battle of the Bocage was a bloody business. The Americans alone lost more than 8,000 killed and 40,000 wounded before they got to Saint Lo. Patton seemed to spend his time going to the funerals of his friends. Among them was his beloved Colonel Paddy Flint, who had rallied his regiment in Sicily by jumping on top of a truck in nothing but a pair of shorts and shouting at the Germans, "Shoot, you so-and-sos. You don't shoot any better than you did in the last war."

After a long wait for favorable weather the breakout attack began on July 25, 1944, with a tremendous aerial and artillery bombardment, followed by a powerful forward thrust of First Army. The shove shattered the left of the German line and opened a narrow corridor between the Nazis and the sea at Avranches. It was a clean breakout, and Eisenhower gave the order that launched Lucky through the hole.

Though Patton had commanded Third Army for five months, he was not formally in command until Bradley gave him the word on July 28; and Third Army was already driving into France when it became officially operational on August 1.

Perhaps the greatest chance any American commander took in the war was sending Third Army through the single coastal road at Avranches, while First Army held off the growing Nazi power like a human dike. A successful counterattack would close the corridor, leaving the finest of all American armies cut off and surrounded. A traffic jam in that narrow gateway to France would have meant a massacre.

Patton said, "It was one of those things that could not be done, but was. I had to say to myself, 'Do not take counsel of your fears.'"

First Army held the line; and to keep Third Army's thousands of vehicles moving at 35 m.p.h., two-star and even three-star generals got off their command cars and directed traffic at critical points like ordinary traffic cops.

Patton was everywhere, screaming, "Hurry! Hurry!"

He found the 6th Armored stacked behind the River Sienne while its staff studied maps. "Why the ——— haven't you crossed?" he shrilled.

"We're looking for a ford."

"I just waded it in two feet of water. One look is worth a hundred reports. Get going!"

One of Patton's cardinal principles was never to stop on the hither side of a river. "Throughout history, wars have been lost through not crossing rivers."

Once out of the corridor, Third Army really began to roll. On August 3 it took Rennes, the capital of Brittany. By August 4 it was going so fast that Patton had temporarily lost touch with 4th Armored. With Stiller leading the way in an armored car, he set out in his jeep with Captain Charles K. Codman, who had replaced Jensen, to find it. They raced through Avranches and Comborg to Medrinac. There they found an excited liaison officer who told them the road ahead was under fire. Patton decided that the "poor boy was touched in the head," and they proceeded "cautiously." For ten miles they did not see a single soldier, American or German; but when they finally found 4th Armored's command post. They learned that they had been driving through territory supposedly held by an enemy division.

That was a glorious week. Before it ended, Brittany was sealed off from France and largely overrun; the 12th and 20th Corps of Third Army moved to the jump-off positions for the drive through France; and 15th Corps doubled back toward the east to trap the Germans, who were attacking the Avranches corridor.

The only way Patton could personally visit his far-flung units was in a Piper Cub, in which he skimmed over the treetops of Brittany and dropped in on surprised commanders. He paid a call on Major General Robert C. Macon, who was besieging Saint-Malo with the 83rd Division.

It was temporarily quiet in that sector, and Patton said, "Let's go a little farther forward."

Macon replied, "General, if you just move up there forty yards you'll be in the enemy front line."

Patton was pretty nervous on these low-level flights. He admitted to feeling like a clay bird in front of a crack trapshooter.

The airboys did nothing to cheer him up. They said, "If the Jerrys don't get you, the Americans will; they're all trigger-happy."

Many people criticized Patton's constant appearances at the front as showing off, but he considered them essential. As he tersely put it, "An army is like a piece of cooked spaghetti—you can't push it; you have to pull it after you."

While Third Army was bursting out all over Brittany, Rommel had launched a desperate Panzer attack to close the Avranches corridor behind them. It was stopped by the heroic determination of First Army. Then Patton's 15th Crops curled around behind the Germans, who in turn, were in a trap. There was only a narrow line of retreat, near the town of Falaise, between Montgomery's British on the north and Third Army. Patton could have taken Falaise and sealed off the German armor; but because that sector had been assigned to the British, Eisenhower, fearing that the Allied armies would shoot each other up, ordered him to halt. Montgomery's army failed to arrive until after a considerable portion of the Nazi Panzers had managed to flee through the Falaise gap and escape.

At this time, August 16, the rest of Third Army was making its historic dash through France. Three Army corps abreast moved it with spearheads flung far out ahead. They raced through country that was thick with Nazi troops who were too demoralized to stop them. It was the epitome of the tactics Patton had long planned. His racing columns followed the roads used by Caesar's legions. "If Caesar chose those routes, they must be good," George said. "And the roads he built are still there."

Third Army's spearheads were often fifty miles or more ahead of the main body. Depending on surprise and speed for safety, they cut right through the enemy-held territory. The tankers exuberantly boasted, "We hold the roads; they hold the shoulders." It was all most unorthodox—until you remembered Stuart's cavalry.

Also Patton had one great advantage over Stuart. He had something called Nineteenth Tac (19th Tactical Air Command, attached to Third Army). Patton wrote: "It was love at first sight between me and Nineteenth Tac." Cooperation between ground and air reached an all-time high. Patton dared to leave the long southern flank of his army unguarded because he trusted Nineteenth Tac to report any dangerous concentration of enemy troops, and because he knew that, should such a danger threaten, the superior speed and mobility of Third Army would enable him to swing and counter it.

It addition, Nineteenth Tac, in their Thunderbolt fighter bombers, made life hideous for the fleeing Nazis. They strafed and bombed and, when their bombs were gone and their guns empty, they dropped their belly tanks on German convoys and sent them up in bursts of flame. The whole wide countryside from Brittany to Paris was marked by thick black columns of smoke from the funerals pyres of German armor and transport. Sometimes the roads were so choked by ruined Nazi vehicles that Patton's tankers had to send bulldozers ahead to clear the way. Rommel was badly wounded by a strafing plane.

On August 25, 1944, the great victories of Third Army were dramatically spotlighted when, almost incidentally to that tremendous forward surge, Paris was liberated.

CHAPTER 18

OUT OF GAS

THE LITTLE SIBERIAN PONIES OF GENGHIS KHAN HAD one tremendous advantage over Patton's powerful and speedy armor. Tanks can't eat grass. Instead, they drink gasoline— thousands upon thousands of gallons a day.

By the time Third Army reached the great fortress city of Metz and the Moselle River, near the northeastern border of France, its supply line from Cherbourg and the beaches of Normandy was 500 miles long. Over the fine white roads of France roared the Red Ball Express—hundreds of trucks careening along at fifty miles an hour, night and day, while the exhausted drivers stayed at their wheels eighteen hours out of twenty-four. It was a feat of supply unparalleled in history, but it wasn't enough.

As the supply of gasoline began to fail and the reserves were used up, Patton became frantic. The Nazi armies in front of him were a mere rabble with guns. The Rhine was just over the horizon, and beyond that stately river glimmered the mirage of final victory. He knew he could grasp it if he could keep going.

But the lifeblood of his armor dropped from a gush to a trickle. Then it dried up.

Once during those heartbreaking days a convoy of food trucks arrived. Patton yelled to Bradley, now commanding Twelfth Army Group, "I'll shoot the next man who brings me food. Give us gasoline; we can eat our belts."

A command decision, made without Patton's knowledge but with Bradley and Eisenhower in complete agreement, deprived him of gas and halted Third Army in front of Metz. Perhaps Patton could have crossed the Rhine had they given him every gallon they had, and used the whole air force to carry it to him. But it would have been a foolish decision for Eisenhower to make. He knew now that the game was in his hands. Germany was defeated. It was only a question of time. Had he halted Montgomery and First Army, and given everything to Patton, Eisenhower would have been risking all on a dazzling but unnecessary gamble. Third Army itself was the stake.

Eisenhower had reliable information that the Nazis still possessed powerful forces in Germany. Had he thrown Third Army into the pot, its 450,000-odd troops might have been lost to a German counterattack.

Eisenhower took a less spectacular, more sensible course. The Allied supply situation was desperate. Cherbourg and the Normandy beaches simply could not handle the 20,000 tons of stuff that the armies needed each day. We had to have another great port—and fast. So Eisenhower reluctantly gave priority of supply to Montgomery, for his drive to Antwerp.

Georgie took the decision hard. He imagined that high politics—appeasing the British—influenced Eisenhower's decision. In his ardor he was blind to the overall view. And to his dying day he believed, as his staff officers still do, that only shenanigans at SHAEF kept him from conquering all Germany in those golden September days.

Third Army headquarters was a bad place to be at the time of the great gas drought. Georgie ordinarily smoked twenty long cigars a day, puffing with such nervous energy that an inch of fire, instead of ash, stood out beyond the end. Now he gave up smoking. That was a hurricane warning. His subordinates, even those he loved best, avoided him if possible. Veterans who feared neither Tiger tanks nor Nazi planes turned pale as they entered his office. Willie, the bull terrier, wisely spent much of his time under the bed.

The reign of terror lasted a week. Then, one day, Georgie casually picked up a cigar and lighted it. A few minutes later anxious scouts reported that he was rough-housing with Willie. Third Army felt lucky again.

CHAPTER 19

BUSTING THE BULGE

PATTON WAS UNABLE TO GET GOING AGAIN UNTIL
November 8. Then he captured Metz and slugged his way to the Saar River in a series of dogged attacks against the miraculously revivified German army. That was a month of fog and rain, which turned the fields into morasses and made the roads like the filling of a chocolate cream pie. Casualties from sickness ran high. One division had 3000 cases of trench foot.

Patton raged at the useless waste of men. "The Germans have good boots. Why haven't we? I told them you can't make a waterproof boot with a turned heel."

The General spent half his time teaching junior officers how to take care of their men, saying, "This is more important for young officers to know than military tactics." He personally supervised the arrangements for drying out the soaking troops in every unit he could find time to visit.

On December 16, 1944, Third Army was poised along the Saar for a break-through attack. Patton planned to crack the Siegfried Line and cut his tanks loose in the level fields west of the Rhine. But he kept one anxious eye over his left shoulder. He didn't like the look of things.

The Allied armies were halted on a line from Switzerland to the sea. In places the line bulged with power, where armies gathered for an offensive. In others it was spread as thin as rationed butter. Patton knew that in the Ardennes region of Belgium and Luxumbourg, on his left, 75 miles of line were held by only three divisions of First Army. His G—2 (Intelligence) reported Nazi armor massing opposite them in the Eifel Forest. He passed the word along to Bradley, who replied that there was no danger as the Germans were using the Eifel as a rest area.

On the night of December 16 Bradley telephoned to Patton in his headquarters at Nancy: "The Germans are attacking toward Saint Vith. I've got to take 10th Armored away from you."

Patton nearly melted the wire with the fury of his protest. It would wreck his offensive.

"Ike said you'd yell your head off," Bradley remarked. "But I've got to do it. This is serious."

That turned out to be an understatement. Somehow von Rundstedt had scraped up a mobile reserve of three new armies. They were fresh, and strong, and magnificently equipped; and they fought fanatically because they knew that this was Germany's final hope, Hitler's last desperate gamble. Out of the dark Schnee-Eifel they charged in their terrible Tiger tanks, looming through the dense fog before anyone knew they were coming.

The outnumbered Americans fought back with such desperate valor that they slowed the attack just enough to prevent a chaotic break-through. The thin line crumbled; one whole division was overwhelmed. But they bought time enough to strengthen the shoulders of the spreading bulge in the line, so that the Nazis were channeled straight ahead.

Eisenhower called his generals to meet him at Verdun on December 19, 1944. They were a solemn crew. The Supreme Commander's usually ruddy face was gray from fatigue and strain. Bradley's wrinkles were deeper than ever, and his eyes had lost their kindly humor. British Air Marshal Tedder looked like a worried gremlin. Patton came in shining splendor, wearing his most ferocious war face.

The briefing was pessimistic. Twenty German divisions, half of them Panzers, had already been identified. They were rolling fast, threatening the great supply base at Liége, in Belgium, and the vital port of Antwerp. As a cheering note, Eisenhower pointed out that the Germans had at least come out from behind their great fortifications. There was opportunity here, as well as danger.

"We ought to have the guts to let the so-and-sos go all the way to Paris," Georgie grated. "Then we'd really chew them up."

Eisenhower smiled affectionately at his old friend. "Our plan is to try to hold them short of the Meuse. Hodges will hold the north side of the penetration. Simpson is sending troops to reinforce him, and Montgomery has promised us a corps. Georgie, can you swing at right angles and attack the south side of the salient toward Bastogne?"

"I'll not only attack," said Georgie. "I'll shove von Rundstedt down Montgomery's throat.

Nobody thought Third Army could shift so fast—not Eisenhower, certainly not von Rundstedt. Patton had known what was coming, and had made his plans. His divisions were already alerted. Within hours they were moving to the north;

within three days they were attacking to relieve the American troops who, surrounded by thrice their number of crack Panzer divisions, were holding the vital road center of Bastogne.

Despite the wonderful speed of his shift, Patton was discouraged. His troops hit the hard mass of the German power, and hardly made a dent. Gains were in yards instead of miles. The weather was incredibly bad. Clouds rested on the ground, spewing rain, blanketing the earth, while on a hundred fields our airmen sat looking dismally at their splendid, useless planes and cursing their impotence. Tanks and trucks and jeeps stuck in the mud. America's enormous technical advantage was almost voided by nature's ill temper.

That was Georgie's low ebb of discouragement. He made the un-Pattonish notation in his diary: "This war can still be lost."

Each night he called his commander-in-chief: "I suppose you're going to fire me, Ike."

"Why should I?"

"I'm going so slow."

"You're going as fast as I expected. Keep it up, Georgie!"

Before the Germans attacked, Patton had ordered his chaplain to write a prayer for clear weather. Now he had it printed and sent to all his army.

"But that was for our offensive," Codman objected.

"The Lord won't mind," said Patton.

The prayer went out on little post cards – 450,000 of them:

> *Almighty and merciful Father, we humbly beseech Thee of Thy great goodness to restrain these immoderate rains with which we have had to contend. Grant us fair weather for battle. Graciously harken to us as soldiers who call upon Thee, that armed with Thy power, we may advance from victory to victory, and crush the oppression and wickedness of our enemies, and establish Thy justice among men and nations. Amen.*

The German meteorologists had promised Hitler three weeks of rain. The American weather wizards agreed with them. So it seemed a miracle when the sun rose in a cloudless sky on the morning of December 23.

Georgie, listening to the sonorous roar of motors as bright wings glittered in the sky and the supply parachutes bloomed over Bastogne, said joyously, "That chaplain of mine makes a powerful prayer."

Aided by the released air power, Third Army drove a narrow corridor through the massed Nazi Panzers to Bastogne on December 26. That was the real end of Hitler's hopes, though the battle raged for four terrible weeks. The blessed sunshine was succeeded by a blinding blizzard that smothered the country under three feet of snow, while a gale from the Siberian steppes brought subzero temperature.

The troops were ill equipped for arctic fighting. They had neither parkas nor shoepacks, nor any white camouflage suits, nor white paint for the tanks. Some of the replacements rushed into the line were so ill trained that they did not know how to put a rifle together. Of them Patton said, "I feel like a murderer."

Patton fought one of his greatest battles with CZ (Communication Zone), to get the stuff they needed. He even hired a French factory to turn out 10,000 white, hooded capes a week. He was hardly ever in his fine headquarters in the city of Luxembourg. An early morning visit to the great war room for a quick glance at the large-scale situation map, and a brief runover of intelligence reports. Then he took to his open jeep, crabbing and jolting over the snow-choked roads to see and be seen by all the troops he could reach. As a matter of principle, Patton always traveled by jeep when going to the front and came back by plane. This was so troops could see their commander going forward, but never see him heading for the rear. However, during the Battle of the Bulge the weather was so bad that planes were out.

Thus it happened that Patton received one of the most cherished tributes of his life. He was returning from the front in the early stages of the engagement when he met the 4th Armored Division moving up. It was a day of utter misery, when air and earth alike seemed liquefied. Vehicles groaned and slithered and bogged down, until the cursing crews put shoulder to tailpiece and heaved them out by mass man power. Though their present state was forlorn, the men of 4th Armored knew that their next condition would be worse. They were about to face the terrible Nazi power in a death grapple in those swirling mists, and virtually every one of them felt the sick stab of fear in his bowels.

Yet, when they recognized the stern and lonely figure sitting in the back of the three-starred jeep, the first echelons raised a shout that echoed across the muddy fields and rolled on down the line. The sight of their general sent a wave of confidence surging through the whole division, and as his jeep passed the tanks and half-tracks, the mobile guns and truckloads of soldiers, their wild cheering was for victory already won because they trusted him.

Years later a soldier who was there that day said to Mrs. Patton, "I knowed your husband well. We was on a truck that had gone into the ditch, when his jeep came up with him standing in the back of it screaming, "Get out of that, you blank-blank sons-of-blanks, and heave her out!"

"We tumbled out fast and began to push. The next thing, I saw that the man pushing alongside of me was the General himself.

Yes, ma'am, I knowed him well!"

Occasionally Patton took a day off to visit Bradley or Eisenhower and express his sulphuric opinion of Montgomery for not attacking more vigorously from his side of the Bulge. Because of poor communications and the need for British troops in the fighting, Eisenhower had put Montgomery in command of all forces, British and American, north of the Bulge.

Inevitably Patton loathed Montgomery. Oddly there were numerous points of resemblance between them. Montgomery was dramatic, eccentric, and dictatorial, like the American. There, however, likeness ended. Montgomery planning a battle was as fastidious as an old maid getting ready for a tea party; everything had to be just so, and in its proper place, before he would move. He totally lacked Patton's magnificent improvisation, and his headlong ardor. Georgie simply could not understand such caution. And he was as jealous as a bride of what he considered SHAEF's partiality for the Englishman.

But Monte got going at last. The German armor slithered back through the narrowing gap between the Allied lines, spitting fire like a wounded dragon. And on January 14 the British 30th Corps made contact with the American 17th Airborne Division at Saint Hubert. The Bulge was flattened; the breach was closed. Third Army gathered itself for the grand final surge that was to carry it from the Saar all the way across Germany to Czechoslovakia with hardly a halt.

CHAPTER 20

A DOZEN CANNAES

AT ALL TIMES PATTON CARRIED THREE CAMPAIGNS IN
his head: the one he was fighting, the next one, and—more neb-
ulously but still forming—the one after that. On the very day
Third Army retook the last sliver of the Bulge, Patton began the
drive that only victory stopped. It was January 29, 1945.

The attack was designed to go through the forested Eifel,
where von Rundstedt had secretly massed his armor before the
Bulge. It was a country of steep hills and dark forests,
quartered by rivers in flood. The hills were strewn with
pillboxes that commanded the rivers, for it was the heart of the
Siegfried Line. The miserable roads had been pulverized by the
frantic ebb and flow of Nazi Panzers. In some places the en-

gineers had to build corduroy roads as they went forward. And the rains were still "immoderate."

As Patton put it, "the attack was very sticky" at first. Crossings were made on the Our and Saure rivers, in assault boats; but thirty-six out of the first thirty-eight boats of the 5th Division were smashed by enemy fire. The troops finally got a bridgehead, but there was no bridge. For several days they clung to their precarious position, supplied by boats and from the air. Then the engineers managed to get a single assault bridge across the Saure.

Patton came down to the river bank the next day. He was determined to visit the troops on the far bank, but the assault bridge was commanded by enemy guns. At his orders a smoke screen was laid down and, followed by Major General Manton S. Eddy, he started across. As they moved cautiously forward, the frail bridge sagged under their weight. Water lapped Georgie's cavalry boots; smoke billowed around, and bullets zipped into the river making his stomach quiver. At midstream the swift current was grappling Patton's waist. He stumbled on something soft underfoot—the body of an American soldier. Feeling for a foothold, he inched around it and forward.

From their foxholes men of the 5th Division saw an incredible apparition rise from the thinning smoke—first a fierce, familiar face under a shining three-starred helmet; then broad shoulders and a chest full of ribbons; finally long, thin legs, dripping and bedraggled.

"Georgie!" they shouted. "Here comes Georgie!"

That was the origin of the story that Patton swam the Saure River. "I didn't swim," he wrote to Bea, "but it would have been easier if I had."

Not all Patton's troubles came from the Nazis and the weather. On February 2 Eisenhower called Bradley, Courtney Hodges of First Army, Simpson, and Patton to confer with him at Spa in Belgium. They met in the same ornate room where, long ago, von Hindenburg told his Kaiser that another war was irretrievably lost. Patton, too, got bad news.

Eisenhower told his general that the Combined Chiefs of Staff, then on their way to Yalta, had decided that the main attack toward the Rhine was to be staged by Montgomery with his Twenty-First Army Group and the American Ninth Army. All other American armies were temporarily to go on the defensive and reinforce Montgomery.

Patton was livid. "What's the defensive?" he demanded. "Nobody ever successfully defended anything. Look at Troy.

Look at Hadrian's Wall. Look at the great Wall of China and the Maginot Line."

"Those are my orders," Eisenhower answered.

"It's ignominious for the Americans to be on the defensive when the war ends," Patton argued. "When will Monte jump off?"

"On February 10."

"Can Hodges and I at least keep attacking until then?"

Eisenhower grinned and nodded.

After that, Patton was very secretive about his plans for fear they might be countermanded. He had one bad day when the Commander-in-Chief summoned him to Bastogne.

"I'll bet Ike's found out about Eddy's attack and is going to stop it," Georgie said gloomily.

But the trip turned out to be only for the purpose of having his picture taken with the other generals in the ruins of Bastogne.

Promptly on February 10 Bradley telephoned Patton to ask when he could go on the defensive.

Patton answered him, with no burst of violent language but in solemn words. "Brad," he said. "I'm the oldest and most experienced commander in the United States Army in Europe. If I have to go on the defensive, I'll ask to be relieved."

"You can't do that, Georgie," Bradley replied. "You owe too much to your troops. You must stay on."

"I am owed a great deal too," Patton said. "Unless I can keep on attacking, I will have to be relieved."

Bradley pondered that. As he spoke his next words, Georgie could almost see the characteristic secret humor light his brown eyes.

"You'll have to go on the defensive; that's orders," said Bradley. "But you can continue to make probing attacks to keep the enemy off balance."

"I understand," said Georgie—and went right on attacking. He called it a "creeping defense."

They had taken the 35th Division for Montgomery. Then they took the 95th. But the attack continued. Every division was kept in action. There was virtually no reserve, but Georgie didn't believe in reserves. "A guy who isn't shooting is wasted," he said.

Patton kept switching his depleted forces back and forth in order to bring the most effective power to bear on the weakest point. This necessitated some dizzy logistics. At one point a corps commander made an error which produced the nightmarish situation of two armored divisions passing through each other at a crossroads at night. The only way to avoid an awful traffic jam was to keep them both rolling, sending alternate vehicles through at high speed. It was dangerous work and an M.P. directing traffic was killed by a speeding tank, under the eyes of the corps commander.

A few minutes later Patton roared up in a jeep. He stormed over to this nervous subordinate and shrilled, "I'm not going to have my M.P.'s killed by your foolishness. You made this mess; now you get out there and direct traffic yourself!"

For nine solid hours that two-star general stood in the crossroads waving the traffic through with an electric torch as the tanks crashed by at 35 m.p.h.

Trier, the key city of the Saar defenses, fell on March 2. By that time all the British and American armies on the north had begun the great sweep forward to the Rhine. On March 5 Patton sent 4th Armored careening off into the heart of the Rhineland. They took a Nazi corps commander and his whole headquarters the next day, and reached the Rhine on March 7.

On that same day First Army got the luckiest break of the war. Its 9th Armored Division captured the Ludendorf Bridge at Remagen, intact, and rushed across to establish a bridgehead on the east bank of the Rhine. Patton records: "We were delighted, but a bit envious."

Following 4th Armored, a dozen divisions of Third Army dashed forward with a whoop, crossing the Moselle, twisting and turning through demoralized German units until they all came up to the Rhine. Patton swung part of his army to the south along the river, cutting off the Nazi armies still fighting Sixth Army Group in the Palatinate as you would snip ivy from its roots.

Hannibal's victory over the Romans at Cannae is considered the classic example of the destruction of an enemy army by double envelopment (encircling it from two sides). Patton's campaign in the Palatinate was a whole series of Cannaes as his divisions circled and met, parted, and circled and met again, engulfing a Nazi army corps at each sweep. In fact, when he met the newspapermen each morning, Georgie would say, with a big grin. "Well, boys, I guess we'll have another Cannae today."

Patton was always extremely conscious of historical parallels. He loved to follow in the footsteps of the great conquerors. When he drove with his armored legions up the old Roman road to Trier, he could almost see the dust clouds and the sparkle of the Roman eagles and "smell the coppery sweat."

"I entered by the same gate Lobienus used," he wrote in high delight.

But, although his tactics were based on classical principles, his execution of them was peculiarly his own. As he once said, "I'm going to be an awful irritation to the military historians, because I do things by a sixth sense. They won't understand."

When the pressure of battle supercharged his genius, that sixth sense enabled Patton to make the lightning decisions that utterly confounded enemy generals by their seeming omniscience. That was the secret of the great Palatinate campaign, where in ten days Patton's army surrounded and destroyed two German armies, captured 60,000 prisoners and 10,000 square miles of territory, with minimum losses.

As Eisenhower had hoped and Patton predicted the Germans were defeated west of the Rhine. They had not enough left to make a real stand on that traditionally inviolable border of their sacred Fatherland.

CHAPTER 21

THE TIDE OF
VICTORY

ON THE FULL TIDE OF VICTORY, ON MARCH 19, 1945, three generals met at Patton's headquarters: Omar Bradley, tall and a little stooped; Courtney Hodges, shorter and stockier, in a characteristically plain uniform with baggy pants; and Patton, wearing a perfectly tailored battle jacket and a firmament of stars, with his six-guns pendent from a broad, tooled leather belt. The three were almost as gloomy as though the enemy had them on the run.

Bradley, commanding Twelfth Army Group (First and Third Armies), was the closest friend Eisenhower had, and completely in his confidence. He set the problem. Looking at the big situation map that covered one wall of Patton's elaborate war room, he said, "Ike has to make the main effort in the north. That's the plan, and he must stick to it. Once Montgomery gets across the Rhine, we'll lose at least ten divisions to him and have to sit down."

Hodges sadly nodded, and Georgie gave an inarticulate snarl.

"But," Bradley said, "Ike's directive that any commander who comes up to the Rhine shall exploit any opportunity to get across gives us an out. If Georgie can get across, then Courtney can break out of the Remagen bridgehead; and we'll get our divisions committed so they can't take 'em away. Can you do it, Georgie?"

"What do *you* think, Brad?"

Up at the northern end of the line, Montgomery had massed the utmost power of all arms for a full-dress amphibious assault. Infantry regiments were crowded like subway riders along the banks of the Rhine, waiting close to the naval landing craft that had been laboriously trucked over the narrow roads. Behind them hundreds of tanks of the armored divisions waited nose to stern for the first bridge to be thrown across the river. The whole wide sweep of plain bristled with heavy artillery like a pin cushion. And on airfields, from Belgium back to northern England, bombers and fighters and transports and gliders were ready for the greatest aerial effort in history, when, in addition to saturation bombing, two complete airborne divisions would be dropped behind the enemy lines. It was a typical Montgomery set-piece attack—a massive power drive. The jump-off was timed for Saturday, March 24, 1945.

On the evening of Thursday, March 22, men of Patton's 5th Division stole silently through the cobbled streets of the little ruined city of Oppenheimer, down to the sheltered barge harbor. There they quietly embarked in a heterogeneous collection of craft, from small assault boats to a few naval landing craft.

At 1:30 A.M. on Friday morning a line of assault boats, with the men dipping their paddles as quietly as Indians on a moose hunt, slipped out onto the broad, black bosom of the German river. Ten minutes later their heels grated softly on the opposite bank. Out of them swarmed troops, scuffling a little, splashing, cursing in whispers, yet all so quietly that no alarm was raised. They spread out in a widening semicircle, moving, crouched, through the wet meadows, choosing positions in which to set the machine guns and mortars and the light cannon they carried.

Behind them came more men—shadows creeping up the bank, settling in thickening clusters in ditches and behind walls. So skillful were they, so unprepared the enemy, that they had twenty precious minutes on the German bank of the Rhine before the first Nazi sentry shouted a startled challenge and fired his rifle.

Give Third Army twenty minutes to effect a lodgment and then try to blast them out! The weak German attack that finally developed was like a snowball fight to the battle-wise 5th Division. Patton was across the Rhine!

Twenty-three hours later, Montgomery's massed guns lighted forty miles of horizon as they blasted out the opening barrage. The airplanes darkened the skies, where parachutes bloomed as thickly as bluebonnets in Texas, and under a rolling smoke screen the crowded landing craft roared across the river.

Patton gleefully listened to a British broadcast—made in advance and released by mistake—in which Churchill congratulated Montgomery on being the first to make an assault crossing of the Rhine. He swore in delight at the British discomfiture, and exuberantly wrestled with Willie.

Then he crossed the Rhine himself. As he landed on the far bank, Georgie deliberately tripped and fell—in imitation of William the Conqueror landing in England. He jumped up holding a handful of German soil.

The crossing of the Rhine was the last real battle. There was plenty of fighting left; many men were uselessly killed, while Hitler still lived to order his fanatical troops to fight to the last. But the German armies were no longer disciplined bodies of men maneuvering in accordance with a coordinated plan. They had become individual units fighting wherever they happened to be—hopeless, suicidal.

Third Army's triumphant rush through the heart of Germany recalled the great days in France. It was almost a mass picnic, with everyone in high spirits. Tanks and trucks and all the heterogeneous vehicles of a mechanized army careered at full speed over the splendid German roads, while farmers unconcernedly plowed their fields and the greatest danger came from the fanatical Hitler Youth—boys from ten years old upward— who, armed with abandoned weapons of the retreating Wehrmacht, shot up isolated groups of Americans.

There were grim moments, too, when Third Army captured the great Nazi concentration camps with their skeleton inmates, their torture rooms and gas chambers, and the piled-up bones of their thousands of victims. Patton personally visited the first of the horror camps at Ohrdruf, forcing himself to walk slowly through the ghastly sights and smells. Then he ordered the German citizens sent there, to see and ponder. When the Nazi Mayor of Ohrdruf and his wife were shown the inside of the camp for the first time, they were so stricken with guilt that they went home and killed themselves.

Other captures were gayer. The 90th Division turned up the whole Nazi gold reserve in a salt mine at Merkers. It consisted of 4,500 gold bricks, each weighing 25 pounds; also suitcases full of wedding rings, gold spectacles, and even teeth pulled from the heads of prisoners for their fillings.

On April 12, 1945, Eisenhower and Bradley arrived, in cub planes, at Patton's new command post at Hersfeld, deep in the heart of Germany. Ike and Georgie spent the whole day together; it was the last such day these two old friends were to know.

They sat up late talking of future plans for the redeployment of their troops in the Pacific. When Georgie went to bed, he turned on the radio to get a time signal. Instead he heard a solemn voice announce the death of President Roosevelt. He hurried over to tell Eisenhower and Bradley. For long hours more, they discussed the passing of their great Commander-in-Chief and what it might mean to the war. They decided that it would not affect the actual drive for victory, but they were oppressed by a tremendous sense of loss—

a curious vacuum. Eisenhower records: "We went to bed depressed and sad."

On May 6, 1945, Third Army had cut Germany in two, crossing the Danube and entering Czechoslovakia. That day 16th Armored took Pilsner, and Third Army patrols were in the vicinity of Prague. A meeting with the Russians was imminent, and Patton arranged to present decorations to Russian officers in return for those he knew they would give Third Army. Since the Russians also loved to exchange personal gifts, such as watches and side arms, Georgie cannily wore his second-best watch and left the famous white pistols in his trailer.

All the other Allied armies had advanced up to the stop-line agreed upon, long in advance, between Eisenhower and the Russians. Hitler made his dramatic farewell to the loyal few in his embattled Bunker in Berlin, and shot himself as the Russian troops fought through the suburbs. News came to Patton that Grand Admiral Karl Doenitz, the new chief of the tattered remnant of the German Reich, had sent Field Marshal Alfred Gustave Jodl to Eisenhower's headquarters at Rheims to negotiate the surrender.

Patton telephoned Bradley that morning: "Brad, can't I go on and take Prague? My patrols are already there."

"No," Bradley replied. "The stop-line is Pilsen-Lenz."

And there they stopped.

In the schoolhouse in Rheims the sullen Germans signed an unconditional surrender. There was no victory celebration at Third Army headquarters that night—they were all too tired. Patton felt let down. The job for which he had been born, toward which he had trained himself for fifty years, was done.

That it was well done, he knew. Third Army had taken more enemy territory and caused more enemy casualties than had any other American army in history. Its losses had been held to an amazing minimum. That to George was the test of generalship. He knew he had passed it.

Patton had passed another test as well—he had won the affection and loyalty of his army. Somewhere on those long, long miles from Normandy to Lenz, the sentiment of the men had changed. They might still curse his discipline and make fun of his theatrics. But they trusted him and would follow him wherever he led—because he *led*. They were inordinately proud of him and jealous of his reputation. And, at the end, it was much more than that. With all his faults they loved him.

CHAPTER 22

THE CONQUEROR
COMES HOME
JUNE 8, 1945

ACROSS THE HOT BLUE SKY OVER BEDFORD, Massachusetts, sang the fighter plans, wing-tip to wing-tip After them droned the Fortresses in bombing formation. Bea, standing with her daughters and son, who had twenty-four hours leave from West Point, in front of the great crowd at the airport, peered impatiently toward the east. Her keen eyes caught the flash of a lone silver wing and never after lost it. Here he came at last!

The fighters and bombers swept on, but the big, four-motored transport slanted down, circled, and rolled up the concrete. Pandemonium broke loose—people were cheering, guns firing, sirens screaming; and the fighters, swinging back, were diving on the field—but Bea, concentrating on the door in the side of the great plane, hardly noticed the noise.

A group of soldiers shoved the landing stage toward it; and before the folding platform touched the side of the ship, the door flew open and Georgie jumped across the gap. For an instant he stood alone, glittering in his stars and ribbons, while a solid roar went up that drowned the guns and planes and sirens. With his polished boots twinkling, he ran down the steps and across the apron to catch Bea in his arms and hug her hard.

Then the welcome caught up with him, and he was swept off in a brassy red fire chief's car—to drive through fifteen miles of shouting crowds to Boston, and more crowds and ceremonies and guns. Patton had a hard time keeping his "war face" on. How he loved his hero's welcome!

That night they were all at Green Meadows. Almost until morning they sat talking. George flung innumerable questions at his father, and the latter answered them until they were both too exhausted to say more. At six o'clock that morning George took off for West Point. It was the last time he saw his father.

The Boston welcome was nothing to that of Los Angeles, which is a city that can really go crazy. There Patton rode, standing in a jeep, through crowds that surged through the police lines and fought to touch the immaculate sleeve of his coat. In the Coliseum that night 100,000 persons came to greet him under the blazing searchlights, and to watch the show they had put on for him. It was a sham tank battle with great, cumbersome armored vehicles wheeling and charging one another in an infernal clangor of howling motors, and barking guns; of exploding land mines, and rockets sizzling across the turf.

Patton watched with a broad grin on his face. When it was over, he said exultantly into the microphones that carried his voice across the nation, "That's the nearest thing to a real battle I've ever seen. And, God help me, I love it!"

Georgie stayed for a few days at Lake Vineyard, in the great stone mansion his father had built when the old adobe ranch house finally crumbled away. Nita was living there, and Bea was with him, and all the family came to see him. It was almost like a fiesta in Don Benito's time. But some of the old people he had loved as a boy were too frail to make the trip, among them his old nurse, aged ninety-five, and Uncle Captain. These he went to see, spending an hour or more with each, teasing them and shocking them delightfully with his rough language.

On Sunday he went with Bea and Nita to the Church of our

Savior at San Gabriel. There, as was fitting, he offered his heart-felt thanks to God—for his great victories, and for helping him to do his best.

On December 9, 1945, a long black limousine rolled down the auto-strada with the dignity befitting a four-star general. Inside it sat General Patton, now commanding Fifteenth Army of the occupation Troops, and his good friend General Gay. They were on their way from headquarters to a pheasant shoot at Mannheim. Patton's beautiful shotgun was in its leather case on the floor. He was looking forward to a pleasant day; and looking further toward a pleasant future. For his orders had come, and in a few days he was going home to Green Meadows.

It happened a few miles from Bad Nauheim. The General's car was going down the auto-strada at about thirty-five miles an hour when Patton said sharply, "Look at that!"

A truck, coming from the opposite direction, pulled across in front of them toward a parking place. Patton's driver tried to swerve left; but his timing was off, that winter morning.

There was a violent crash as the limousine hit the truck almost head-on. Patton was flung against the front seat and landed in a heap on the floor.

To the men who leaped out of the truck and gathered

around the General's car, it didn't look as though anyone were seriously hurt. General Gay and the driver were preparing to get out, and General Patton, though crumpled in a heap on the floor, was perfectly conscious.

Only Georgie knew better. When the crash had snapped him violently forward, he felt something crack. He was not very badly bruised, but the stiff old neck, which had never bent to anyone but God, was broken.

Almost casually, as though remarking on a purely impersonal event, George Patton spoke to Gay. "This is a hell of a way to die."

Twelve days later, on December 21, 1945, General George Smith Patton, Jr., died. Bea was with him, fighting for him through his illness. As was his way, Georgie put up a terrific fight against his last antagonist. It was the only battle he ever lost.

One of Patton's strong beliefs was that a solider should lie where he falls. So, according to his wish, he was buried in the military cemetery at Hamm, in Luxembourg, among 30,000 men who fought for him.

Even though he lies so quietly in the soil he conquered, George Patton is still, as ever, the center of a raging controversy.

Should he have been allowed to close the gap at Fallaise? Could he have crossed the Rhine in September, 1944? Was he a great strategist, or merely a superb tactician and a magnificent leader of men? What manner of man was he anyhow, a hard-boiled brute or a warmhearted old curmudgeon?

The arguments range in the officers' clubs from Manila to Vienna. They resound through the Pentagon at odd intervals. And in barrooms and general stores his ex-GI's bicker back and forth. The controversies will go down through history until the last book is written.

For Georgie Patton lived so furiously that people could not judge him calmly. No one merely liked him. Either they adored him with the flaming loyalty that his own men gave him, or they hated his liver and lights.

Nearly always they misunderstood him; for he was like a storm center whirling through his world, raising dust and debris that blinded the eyes of men. With his tirades and his tears he seemed utterly contradictory—yet he was completely consistent; for he was almost unduly sensitive, and that tough shell was a magnificent bluff.

General Eisenhower, who really understood him, said, "Patton's besetting sin was softheartedness."

In regard to his reputation as a soldier, there is one voice that speaks without prejudice—and surely with competent knowledge. So let Patton's greatest enemy pronounce his military epitaph.

This is Field Marshal Karl Gerd von Runstedt, Commander-in-Chief of all the German armies in France and in the Battle of the Bulge. He is talking to Patrick Mitchell, correspondent in Germany for the *Stars and Stripes*, after the surrender. The question concerns the quality of the American generals.

Spitting out the unfamiliar English words with great emphasis, the doomed Nazi marshal makes his unbiased pronouncement: "Patton, he iss your best!"

Index

ABOUT THE AUTHOR

Born in 1898, ALDEN HATCH spent much of his life on crutches. He had tuberculosis of the bone, a disease that came and went away all during his lifetime. He always considered this a blessing, though, because he was introduced to books and writing at a very early age.

Mr. Hatch received most of his schooling at home and even earned a law degree by mail from the University of Chicago. His health recovered enough when he was a young man so that he was able to travel and enjoy activities such as tennis and horseback riding. He even rode a camel through the Sahara Desert!

Writing was Mr. Hatch's real passion, though, and he started by writing short stories for magazines. Soon he found his true calling—writing biographies. Over the course of his life he met and interviewed dozens of world leaders, movie stars, and politicians. He wrote thirty-six biographies and counted many of his subjects as his friends.

BOOKS IN THIS SERIES

✷ STERLING POINT BOOKS

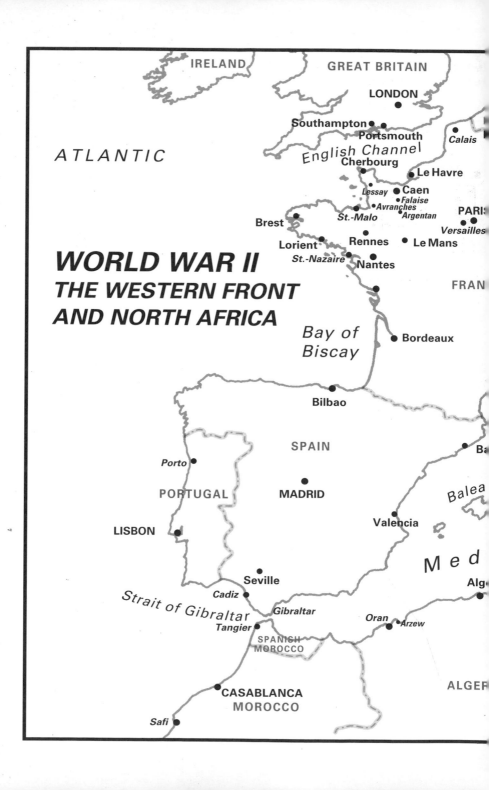